HOW TO PRUNE
FRUITING PLANTS

HOW TO PRUNE FRUITING PLANTS

A practical gardener's guide to pruning and training tree fruit and soft fruit, with easy-to-follow advice and over 300 step-by-step photographs

RICHARD BIRD

southwater

Dedication
To Hilary with lots and lots of love

This edition is published by Southwater, an imprint of Anness Publishing Ltd, Blaby Road, Wigston, Leicestershire LE18 4SE; info@anness.com

www.southwaterbooks.com; www.annesspublishing.com

If you like the images in this book and would like to investigate using them for publishing, promotions or advertising, please visit our website www.practicalpictures.com for more information.

Publisher: Joanna Lorenz
Project Editor: Molly Perham
Designer: Michael Morey
Jacket Design: Bally Design Associates
Illustrator: Liz Pepperell
Production Controller: Steve Lang

© Anness Publishing Ltd 2013

A CIP catalogue record for this book is available from the British Library.

Bracketed terms are intended for American readers.

PUBLISHER'S NOTE
Although the advice and information in this book are believed to be accurate and true at the time of going to press, neither the authors nor the publisher can accept any legal responsibility or liability for any errors or omissions that may have been made nor for any inaccuracies nor for any loss, harm or injury that comes about from following instructions or advice in this book.

Contents

Introduction

Pruning increases the productivity of fruit trees and bushes and improves their shape. The very act of pruning involves looking closely at the plant, so you are likely to be much more aware of any problems. You can then take avoiding action by cutting out dead and diseased wood, which helps keep a plant in tip-top condition. Pruning and training plants also prevents the branches from becoming overcrowded so that more air and light can enter, again helping to maintain a healthy plant.

Basic pruning techniques

Although different fruit trees and bushes may need different pruning techniques, the physical process of making the cuts is usually the same. Cuts are generally made with secateurs (pruners), or long-handled pruners for thicker growth, or a saw of some kind. There are several general principles that apply when you are using all types of pruning

ABOVE Pear trees can be left to grow as standard trees, but they look better and are more manageable if pruned into bushes, pyramids, espaliers or, as here, a fan trained against wires.

equipment. The first may seem obvious, but it is often overlooked. The cut must be clean and there should be no tears in the wood or bits left hanging around the cut. The one essential requirement for achieving this, besides the ability to use the tools properly, is for the tools to be sharp and well maintained. A pair of secateurs that crushes the wood, rather than cleanly cutting through it, can cause problems.

When pruning trees, be aware that branches can be heavy, so avoid cutting straight through one in such a way that the weight makes it fall before you have finished cutting, tearing back along the branch or even down the trunk.

Avoid snags

The second basic principle is to avoid snags. Snags are the short pieces of wood that stick out beyond a branch or a bud. All cuts should be made tight against the stem or up to

a bud if removing the end of a shoot. Any piece of wood sticking out will not only look ugly but will usually die back, leaving dead wood through which diseases can enter.

Ends of shoots or branches

When you are removing the end of a shoot or a branch, a sloping cut should be made just above the nearest bud to the point at which you want to shorten the shoot. The cut should be sloped at 45 degrees away from the bud (be careful not to cut through the bud). If you do accidentally cut through the bud, it may be necessary to recut back to the

THE PRUNING CUT
Slope the cut away from the bud, to allow water to drain away and reduce the risk of it rotting the bud.

ABOVE Most people relish the idea of growing their own fruit. Pruning is part of the process and can help improve crops.

next bud. If there are two buds opposite one another, make the cut directly across the stem just above the pair of buds.

Removing a branch or stem

Always cut off a branch or heavier stem with three cuts. This will help prevent the branch splitting. The first cut is made some way out (about 30cm/12in or so) from the trunk, in an upward direction, about a third of the way through. The second is made 8cm (3in) further away from the trunk and in a downward direction. As you pass the initial cut the branch will sag and split along to the second cut but will go no further. You can now cut straight through the remaining stub, close to the trunk.

Sealing wounds

Argument has raged for many years as to whether larger cuts should be sealed with some form of compound. Although some gardeners still stick to the practice, most now feel it is best to leave all cuts open to the air and weather. Trim round the cut with a sharp knife to remove any rough bark.

Tools and equipment

These can be divided into four groups. There are those that perform the cuts, such as saws, secateurs (pruners) and knives; those that are used for clearing up, such as rakes, forks and shredders; safety equipment; and finally the means to gain access to taller plants, such as ladders and towers. They can further be divided into manual tools and mechanical ones, such as hedge trimmers and chainsaws.

The most essential tool is a good pair of secateurs. These should be kept sharp. Poor-quality ones, with

ABOVE Ladders can be used for simple tasks such as picking fruit, but more sustained and complicated work is best carried out on a platform.

blades that move apart when you cut, or blunt ones, will tear the wood as it passes through. They may also crush and bruise the wood. To a skilled user, a sharp knife can replace secateurs in certain instances. For thicker wood, a pair of long-handled pruners – secateurs with long handles – can be used, but you should avoid cutting through very thick wood; use a saw instead. Long-arm pruners are secateurs on an extension arm that can reach into tall shrubs or trees but are operated from ground-level.

Saws come in a variety of shapes and sizes. Small folding saws are the most useful type for the small garden owner. These are usually very sharp and remain so for some years. Instead of sharpening, as one used to do, it is usual to buy a new one when it begins to blunt. Bow saws and even chainsaws may be necessary in larger gardens. Some of the folding saws can be attached to extension arms so that higher branches can be removed without the need for ladders.

Power tools

In small gardens it may not be necessary to use power tools, but in a larger one they can be a real boon. The crucial thing is to use them sensibly. Make sure you know how to operate them and that you are well protected. If you are uncertain about your abilities, have any work that entails their use done by professionals. Chainsaws are probably the most dangerous tool and should be used only if you have taken a course on their use. It is also important to keep power tools in good condition. They should be maintained professionally at least once a year. The settings and running of the engine should be checked and the cutters sharpened. Do this ahead of when you will next need them.

You can get power secateurs but these are very expensive and useful only if you have a large orchard and have a lot of fruit pruning.

Clearing up

Most tools needed for this, such as rakes, brooms, forks, wheelbarrows and carrying sheets, should be part

ABOVE One or more legs can sink into the ground, toppling the stepladder, but special pads will prevent this.

LEFT Shredders are invaluable for recycling prunings of various sizes. Instead of being burnt, they are cut into small enough pieces to be composted and used again in the garden.

of the general garden toolkit. Another piece of power equipment of general use to the pruner is the shredder, which will reduce all the waste to small pieces suitable for composting or mulching. Electrically powered equipment is cheaper but less powerful and less manoeuvrable; petrol-driven machines tend to be heavier but are more mobile and suitable for larger gardens.

You also need to exercise discretion if you opt to burn prunings. Bonfires should be lit at dusk and must be supervised at all times. Check with your local council to see if there are any legal restrictions on bonfires in your area.

Reaching up

There is a limit to how high you can safely reach, especially if you are using power tools. Stepladders can be used for picking fruit as long as the ground is even beneath their feet. They can tip over if you lean out too far, but they do not lean into and deform the plant you are pruning. Ladders can slip sideways and should always be used with care: always face

the ladder into the centre of the tree. It is safer to use a tower scaffold of some description. These are stable and stand on four adjustable legs, and some have wheels so they can be moved around. However, they are bulky, can be cumbersome to move when erected, and you will need somewhere to store them. Chainsaws are now available on extension arms so that you don't have to climb.

Safety equipment

Observing safety precautions is very important. The operator should always be fully protected, with ear protectors, goggles, hard hat, gloves and boots with steel toecaps. A hard hat that includes a face shield and ear protectors is a good idea. When you are wearing ear protectors, someone may approach you undetected, so always keep a sharp eye out. If your hat takes a heavy knock from a branch, replace it, as the impact may have impaired its strength. Providing bystanders with safety equipment should not prove necessary, as they should be kept well out of harm's way at all times.

BASIC TOOLS AND EQUIPMENT

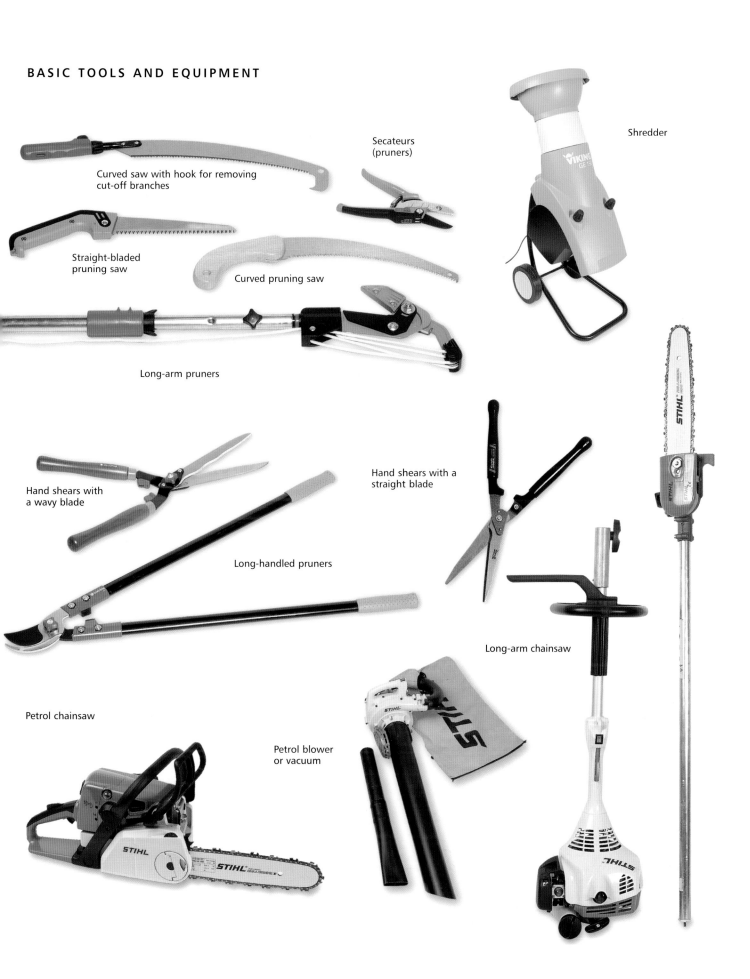

Curved saw with hook for removing cut-off branches

Secateurs (pruners)

Shredder

Straight-bladed pruning saw

Curved pruning saw

Long-arm pruners

Hand shears with a wavy blade

Hand shears with a straight blade

Long-handled pruners

Long-arm chainsaw

Petrol chainsaw

Petrol blower or vacuum

Fruit Trees

Fruit trees have been grown since gardens were first cultivated. Simple pruning has always been undertaken to make fruit trees as productive as possible. However, in recent times, different rootstocks have been produced to control the size and shape of the tree, and with that new methods of pruning have been devised that increase control over the tree and its fruiting capacity. So, now, instead of a normal tree that would take up all of a small garden, you can choose from a variety of shapes, from poles to fans. These can be grown as free-standing trees or trained against walls or fences, or even planted in pots. Now anyone can grow a fruit tree, even with only a balcony.

Although pruning a fruit tree initially appears very daunting, once you have become more familiar with the process, it becomes second nature. Bear in mind that you only need acquire those techniques which apply to the trees you have. However, ignore them and the trees will soon become overgrown and the amount and quality of fruit considerably reduced.

You can simply buy any tree and plant it, but after a few years the results can be disappointing. However, if you learn to prune your trees and attend to them regularly they will provide a lifetime's supply of fruit, well repaying your original investment. The following pages show a range of ways to train and prune various types of hardy fruit tree.

LEFT There is great satisfaction to be gained from growing your own apples: nothing tastes quite so sweet as your own fruit that has been freshly picked from the tree.

Fruit tree shapes

While the typical mental image of a tree is usually a large plant with a solid trunk and a rounded system of branches, there is also a wide variety of forms in which fruit trees in particular can be trained.

Size

There are several reasons for choosing a particular shape of fruit tree. The first is size. A fully grown apple tree, for example, can take up a lot of space, especially in a small garden, but a dwarf pyramid can be fitted into a limited space, while cordons can be grown along a fence or even as a hedge.

Productivity and quality

The second reason for training fruit trees is for improved productivity and quality. A fan grown against a wall will not only produce a large crop but will supply individual fruits with the maximum amount of light for even ripening. The upper branches of a standard tree can shade the lower branches, and these in turn will shade the ground beneath it, limiting what you can grow there. A free-standing fan or cordons that are trained against wires will be far less limiting. Training trees against

ABOVE Espaliered fruit trees are decorative as well as productive and can be used to create effective screens between areas of the garden.

walls also provides protection and warmth for more tender fruits such as peaches or nectarines.

More varieties

When choosing the shape of your tree you should also think about the number of varieties you require. For example, a fan might occupy the whole of one wall, but in the same amount of space you could grow half a dozen cordons or more. These will not necessarily yield more fruit but

could provide variety, giving you a lot more choice in terms of flavour and timing of harvest.

Decorative qualities

Do not overlook the decorative aspect of trained fruit trees. A tall pear espalier growing against the end of a house can be stunning, as can fans on a smaller scale. Free-standing cordons and espaliers produce excellent screens, and can be used as dividers in a kitchen garden.

Choosing trees

Before buying a tree consider the above aspects and think about where you are going to plant it and what the best shape is for the space available. It is also worth bearing in mind that basic shapes, such as standards, require far less pruning than more complicated ones. Something that is often forgotten is that the fruit on larger forms may be out of reach, so if you are not happy on ladders or steps, then these are not for you.

ABOVE Fans are a decorative form which look particularly good when grown against walls. They look attractive, both in blossom and in fruit.

ABOVE Fruit trees can be grown in containers. Here, pear trees have been trained in the form of multiple cordons in terracotta pots.

ABOVE Pole apples are a relatively new introduction. They are particularly suitable for small gardens because they take up little space.

FRUIT TREE SHAPES

The shapes of your fruit trees should be chosen according to their suitability for your available garden space. The more decorative shapes are again dependent on space, but are also a matter of personal preference with regard to how they fit in with the design of the garden as a whole. Obviously, the larger decorative shapes will produce more fruit.

BUSH TREE This is the most practical "tree" shape for most domestic gardens. The size is not too large, making it relatively easy to pick the fruit as well as to carry out pruning.

STANDARD This is the largest of the fruit tree shapes and is not often grown these days. Standards are very large, open trees that need ladders to access them.

SEMI-STANDARD This is similar to a standard except it is smaller. They still need ladders to reach the fruit and for pruning. They have the advantage of looking like a "tree".

SPINDLE BUSH A small, bush-like fruit tree that has its branches spaced for maximum light. Most can be reached from the ground, although taller ones need steps.

DWARF PYRAMID The smallest of the tree shapes and eminently suitable for a small garden. Fruit can be reached and pruning can done from the ground.

FAN This a very good fruit tree shape for walls, fences or even free-standing wirework. Fans are highly decorative and can also be very productive.

CORDON This takes up very little space and can be surprisingly productive. A row of different varieties can easily be accommodated in a small garden.

DOUBLE CORDON This is similar to a cordon, but is upright and has two main stems. Double cordons are obviously more productive than single ones.

POLE This is rather like a single cordon except that it can be much taller. Poles are very useful for small gardens and some can be grown in containers.

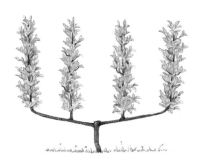

MULTIPLE CORDON This is very similar to the double cordon except that it has four or five upright stems. These can look very decorative, especially once they have aged.

ESPALIER This is one of the most productive of the more decorative shapes. If used against the end of a house, it can produce enough tiers to reach the eaves.

STEPOVER A delightful way of growing apples and pears, making good edging for paths or for dividing areas. In essence, it is a one-tiered espalier.

Rootstocks

There is much more than meets the eye in the production of a fruit tree. While most other plants are grown from seed or by some vegetative means, such as cuttings or division, this does not apply to apples and many other fruit trees. The only way to propagate them is to graft a bud or cutting on to a rootstock. Always check with your supplier before buying a fruit tree that it is on a rootstock suitable for your needs.

A matter of size

The type of rootstock will determine the characteristics of your tree. The graft or scion will determine the type of tree (e.g. 'Bramley' or 'Golden Delicious'), while the rootstock will determine the vigour and hence the ultimate size of the tree. Much research has been carried out into rootstocks and there is an increasing number of them. Until relatively recently, for example, cherry trees could only be grown on non-dwarfing stock and were often very large.

PLANTING A FRUIT TREE

1 Thoroughly prepare the earth, both around the position of the hole and in the bottom of the hole itself. Add plenty of well-rotted organic matter.

2 Check that the rootball is not pot-bound and the roots are not tangled. If they are tangled, gently tease them out, handling them as little as possible.

3 Place the young tree into the hole and check that the surrounding soil is approximately level with that in the container. Do not put the graft below ground.

4 Knock a post in at an angle to avoid damaging the roots. Cut off any extra, so that it does not present a hazard.

5 Firmly secure the tree to the post, using a proper tree tie. Do not use string or anything that can cut into or chafe the trunk.

6 The tree is now ready for its initial pruning. The shape should be rectified to ensure that it grows evenly. The ground should be mulched.

ABOVE An apple on M9 rootstock, which is a dwarfing stock suitable for many bushes and decorative forms in the small garden.

ABOVE An apple on M26 rootstock, a semi-dwarfing stock that can be used for slightly larger decorative forms, like fans and espaliers.

ABOVE An apple on M27, which is the smallest of the rootstocks, used for dwarf pyramids, cordons and other restricted-size forms.

Other qualities

As well as determining final size and shape, rootstocks also influence resistance to pests and diseases. Certain rootstocks are also more suited to certain conditions. Some are more tolerant of drought or can stand cold weather better. In general, one need not worry much about these aspects, as trees sold in your area will probably be suited to local conditions. But bear this in mind if ordering from a nursery.

Planting

In general, fruit trees are sold as "whips", which have a single, upright stem, or "feathered", which have developed side shoots. Planting fruit trees is basically no different from planting any other tree. The ground should be thoroughly prepared and drainage improved if there is the chance that the planting hole will turn into a sump which will retain water. It is important to ensure that the tree is planted at the correct depth. If the junction between the rootstock and the scion is below ground, then the scion is likely to produce suckers that will produce a tree much larger and more vigorous than you had hoped. So, it is important to ensure that the graft is above ground. Make certain that the correct support is in place before planting and then tie in the tree to it.

GRAFTED ROOSTOCKS
This is the rootstock of a grafted fruit tree, showing the junction between the rootstock and the scion, which will form the basis of the tree.

Apple rootstocks

M27	extreme dwarfing stock	bush tree, dwarf pyramid, cordon
M9	dwarfing stock	bush tree, dwarf pyramid, cordon
M26	semi-dwarfing stock	bush tree, dwarf pyramid, cordon
MM106	semi-dwarfing stock	bush tree, spindle bush, cordon, fan, espalier
M7	semi-dwarfing stock	bush tree, spindle bush, cordon, fan, espalier
M4	semi-vigorous stock	bush tree, spindle bush
MM4	vigorous stock	standard
M2	vigorous stock	standard
MM111	vigorous stock	semi-standard, standard, large bush, large fan, large espalier
M25	vigorous stock	standard
MM109	vigorous stock	standard
M1	vigorous stock	standard

Pear rootstocks

Quince C	moderately dwarfing stock	bush tree, cordon, dwarf pyramid, espalier, fan
Quince A	semi-vigorous stock	bush tree, cordon, dwarf pyramid, espalier, fan
Pear	vigorous stock	standard, semi-standard

Cherry rootstocks

Tabel/Edabritz	dwarfing stock	bush tree
Gisela 5	dwarfing stock	bush tree
Colt	semi-vigorous stock	semi-standard
GM61.1	semi-vigorous stock	semi-standard
Mazard	vigorous stock	standard
Mahaleb	vigorous stock	standard

Plum, gage and damson rootstocks

Pixy	dwarfing stock	bush tree, pyramid
Damas C	moderately vigorous stock	bush tree
St Julien A	semi-vigorous stock	bush tree, fan, pyramid
Brompton A	vigorous stock	semi-standard, standard
Myrobalan B	vigorous stock	semi-standard, standard

Apricot, peach and nectarine rootstocks

St Julien A	semi-vigorous stock	bush tree, fan
Brompton A	vigorous stock	bush tree
Peach seedling	vigorous stock	standard, bush tree
Apricot seedling	vigorous stock	standard, bush tree

Basic techniques

As with most aspects of gardening, there are many ways of achieving the same end when it comes to pruning fruit trees. However, there are certain basic rules which apply, especially in connection with how the tree bears fruit.

Basic cuts

The general rules of good pruning apply as much to fruit trees as they do to ornamental ones. Cuts on both smaller shoots and larger branches should be close to a bud or junction so that no die-back occurs on the "snag" (the piece beyond the bud). If you cut between two buds, the section above the remaining bud will invariably die and may cause more extensive problems. The cut should gently slope away from the bud.

The second point to remember is that large branches are heavy, so if you cut straight through one from above, as you approach the bottom of the cut the weight of the branch will cause it to fall and tear back beyond the cut, potentially causing certain problems. Always make a cut

ABOVE It is often necessary to thin out some of the foliage on a fig bush in order to expose the developing fruit to sufficient sunlight to ripen well.

on the underside of the branch first, then make the downward cut. When the branch falls it will now only split as far as your undercut. Once the branch is removed, you can trim back the stub.

The jury is still out as to whether to paint the larger cuts with a sealant. It was once a widespread practice and then became frowned upon, but has been partially revived by some growers in recent years.

ABOVE Upright posts should be knocked into the ground before the tree is planted as they will break the roots if inserted later.

ABOVE If the crop is heavy, you may need to thin out some of the apples in mid-summer to allow the remainder to develop properly.

ABOVE Cutting back the new growth on a pear to reduce its vigour and to promote the formation of fruiting spurs.

ABOVE Spur-bearing fruit trees. Some apple trees produce fruit on older wood and this is normally pruned to form clusters of spurs.

ABOVE Tip-bearing fruit trees. Other trees produce their fruit on the tips of the shoots and must be pruned in such a way that these are not removed.

With so much controversy surrounding the practice, you can make your own choice. The simplest way, which appears as sound as any, is to make clean cuts and leave them alone, apart from paring round the wound with a knife to tidy up any jagged bark.

Initial training
During the first few years after planting it is important to train the tree so that it assumes the desired shape. The basic shape of a cordon might be simple but that of a large fan may take a number of years to complete. Even the less obviously contrived forms such as standards and bushes need initial attention, as they are not quite as natural-growing as they look. These need well-spaced branches and open centres if all the fruit is to have equal access to light and air.

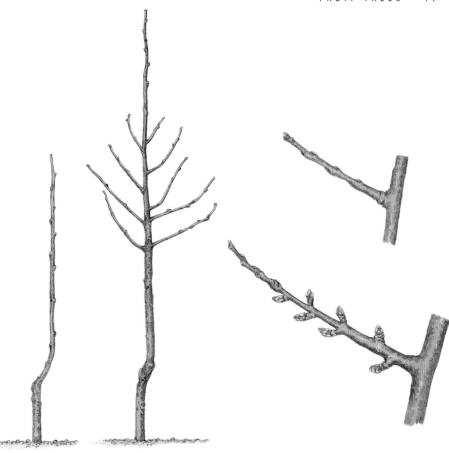

MAIDEN WHIP
In the first year only the main stem develops above the graft. Trees sold in this form are known as maiden whips.

FEATHERED WHIP
During the second or subsequent years the maiden whip produces side shoots and is known as a feathered whip.

LATERALS OR SIDE SHOOTS
(*top*)
This is a new lateral or side shoot with just one year's growth.

(*above*) This is the same lateral in its second year, showing the old and new wood.

Blossom and fruit
Which parts of the plant carry blossom and then fruit varies according to type, and this has a direct bearing on how trees are pruned. For example, most apples produce fruit on short shoots, usually occurring in clusters called spurs. These are usually three years old or more. On the other hand, some varieties produce fruit towards the tips of longer shoots. It follows that the removal of longer shoots in the case of tip bearers would reduce the crop. This is why tip bearers such as 'Worcester Permain' apple cannot be trained as cordons, as the pruning required to maintain the shape would entail removing the fruiting wood. Some trees (e.g. fruiting sour cherries and peaches)

produce fruit only on the previous year's growth, so have to be pruned to encourage plenty of new growth.

General pruning
As well as pruning for fruit, it is also important to consider the general shape of the tree. Any dead or damaged branches should be removed. Along with these, any weak growth, or branches that cross over others, rubbing or crowding them, should be cut out.

Timing
Timing varies according to the type of fruit and the method of training. Generally, standard and bush fruit only need pruning once a year, while the more complex shapes, such as fans, need pruning twice a year.

Renovating fruit trees

If trees are looked after well and pruned regularly, they will continue to fruit freely for many years. However, you may sometimes inherit trees that have been neglected for a variety of reasons or you may not have been as diligent as you might have, and the trees become overgrown and congested. In such cases, the trees do not fruit as prolifically as they once did and those fruits that are carried are much smaller than they should be and are often diseased.

Past it

Not all fruit trees are worth renovating. If they are very ancient, diseased and/or broken, they are best removed and replaced with new ones. If you want to use the tree for shade only, rather than as a fruiting specimen, then it may have a few years of life left in it, but there is always the danger that it may suddenly collapse, causing damage to other plants and possibly even injuring somebody.

First year

It is best to stagger renovation over a period of two to three years so that the tree has a chance to recover from each stage and does not get over-stressed. The first thing to do – as with all pruning jobs – is to look for any dead wood and remove it. At the same time, cut out any dead, diseased, or damaged wood. This will not impose any stress on the tree, so you can go further in the first year. The next problem to tackle is overcrowding. Firstly, you will need to take out any branch that crosses any other branch, especially if it rubs against it. Stand back and assess the tree, noticing whether there is any over-crowding. If necessary, remove some of the branches, especially in

RENOVATING A FRUIT TREE

1 Sometimes a fruit tree can become overgrown, usually through neglect. This is not only unsightly, but it also reduces the tree's productivity.

2 The first task when renovating is to cut out all the dead, diseased or damaged wood. Next, take out any of the older wood that is causing congestion or rubbing other branches.

3 Take out all the "suckers" – new, straight growth, which, if it is allowed to develop, will make the crowding and unproductivity of the tree worse.

4 Cutting back the new growth in this way will encourage new fruiting spurs to develop and increase the tree's fruiting potential.

5 The centre of the tree should now be opened up slightly, so that it is not too crowded and light can enter. This will improve the ripening of the fruit.

6 The same tree the following summer showing the vigorous growth as a result of the renovation. It will need further pruning in spring to contain it.

SPUR-THINNING FRUIT TREES

It is important after a few years to ensure that spurs do not become too crowded, as this will cause a drop in the amount and quality of the fruit being produced. It then becomes important to thin them.

BEFORE PRUNING Once a tree has been bearing fruit for a number of years, the clusters of spurs can become very crowded and productivity can drop.

AFTER PRUNING Reduce the number of spurs by cutting out a number of the older ones, leaving enough to produce the following autumn's fruit.

ABOVE Rows of well-maintained trees in an orchard. Note how pruning has kept the centre of the trees open.

the middle of the tree, so that light can enter and air circulate. If there is a lot to be removed, concentrate on the centre for the first year and thin round the periphery the following year. By now the tree should be beginning to look less neglected and will have gone some way to recovering its proper shape.

Below the tree

If you have a neglected tree, it is important to deal with the ground beneath as well as pruning it. Clear away any brambles and other tough growing weeds. Lightly fork the ground and add plenty of garden compost, manure or other fertilizer. Top-dress with a mulch to improve its moisture-retentiveness. Apply the mulch in a doughnut-like ring around the trunk, making sure it does not touch the trunk. Contact could lead to rotting and/or the production of suckers.

Second year

The shape of the tree has been improved overall, and now it is time to improve the fruiting. Thin out overcrowding around the edges of the tree, if this was not done in the first year. Also, remove much of the new upright growth from the main branches, so that the tree presents a "clean" look. (These whippy growths are often known as "suckers" due to their similarity in appearance to the true suckers that appear from the ground.) Shorten growth at the ends of the branches, cutting back to a replacement bud. The clusters of fruiting spurs are likely to be overcrowded and these will need thinning.

PRUNING A YOUNG PEAR TREE

1 The best way to avoid the need to renovate fruit trees is to start pruning correctly from an early age. Here, young pear trees are being prepared.

2 The central leader of the young pear tree is removed so that the tree bushes out rather than growing tall and lanky.

3 The longer laterals or side shoots are cut back by about half so that they branch, thus creating a well-balanced fruit tree.

4 The shorter laterals towards the top of the leader should now be cut back to a growth bud.

5 Side shoots that are not required for the main structure of the tree should be tipped to encourage fruiting spurs to develop.

APPLES (*Malus domestica*)
Apple standard and semi-standard

The apple standard used to be the preferred type of tree for most commercial growers and for many gardeners. They have fallen out of favour because they take up a great deal of space, besides being awkward to prune, spray, net and pick. However, they still have their devotees, as in the garden they cast incomparable shade for sitting under. The semi-standard, a shorter version, is not so vigorous and has much to recommend it. Both types are free-standing trees. To the uninitiated they can look like unpruned natural trees, so fit in well with many garden settings.

Supports
Drive a stout stake into the ground before planting the tree (doing it after planting risks damage to the roots). In exposed positions, a stake on either side is more secure. Attach to the tree with proprietary tree ties (not string or old nylon tights, which can dig into the bark).

Initial training
Start with a feathered tree, staked. As it grows, gradually remove the lowest side branches to create a bare trunk. Continue to do this until the

ABOVE The medium-size fruit of the apple 'Katja' is best eaten straight from the tree because it quickly loses its flavour.

trunk has reached the required height. Now remove the leader. The main branches then develop from this point and any remaining branches on the trunk can be removed. Ensure that the branches are well spread and remove any that

cross. Shorten the shoots that develop on these branches so that the tree branches out. Keep the centre of the tree open.

Established pruning
Usually only winter pruning is required for standards. The method depends on whether the variety is spur-bearing or tip-bearing. On the former, remove any excessively vigorous and/or badly placed wood, along with any branches that are crossing or rubbing. The leaders of all branches can be reduced by one-quarter to one-third of the previous season's growth. Check the spurs: if any are overcrowded, remove the older and less productive wood. On tip-bearers, either leave the young wood unpruned or just remove the tip back to a bud. Take out older wood back to young shoots to ensure renewal and continued fruiting. Again, also take out any crossing or rubbing branches as well as any that are too vigorous or are misplaced. In both cases try to keep the centre reasonably open.

ABOVE 'Laxtons' Epicure' apples. There are lots of varieties of apple available to gardeners that cannot be bought at the supermarket.

Varieties

Dessert	
'Blenheim Orange'	'Laxton's Fortune'
'Braeburn'	'Laxton's Superb'
'Cox's Orange	'Lord Lambourne'
Pippin'	'Millers Seedling'
'Discovery'	'Ribston Pippin'
'Egremont Russet'	'Starking'
'Fuji'	'Sturmer Pippin'
'Gala'	'Worcester
'George Cave'	Pearmain'
'Golden Delicious'	
'Granny Smith'	**Cooking**
'Idared'	'Bramley's Seedling'
'James Grieve'	'Grenadier'
'Jonagold'	'Howgate Wonder'
'Jonathan'	'Lord Darby'
	'Newton Wonder'

TRAINING AN APPLE STANDARD

There is not a great deal to do when training a standard or semi-standard apple. However, the training that is required is very important because the initial structure will be with the tree for life unless branches become diseased or damaged. Both tip- and spur-bearers are started in the same way, but they are treated differently from the third year onwards.

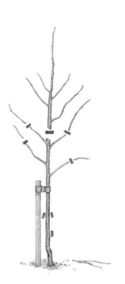
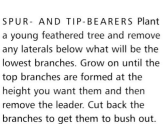

SPUR- AND TIP-BEARERS Plant a young feathered tree and remove any laterals below what will be the lowest branches. Grow on until the top branches are formed at the height you want them and then remove the leader. Cut back the branches to get them to bush out.

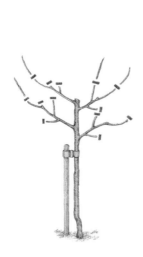

SPUR- AND TIP-BEARERS As the tree develops, remove any sub-branches that cross over or rub against each other, cut back new growth on the main branches by half, and cut back any side shoots not required as branches to about four buds.

SPUR-BEARERS Once the fruit tree is established, cut back new shoots to about five buds. Continue to remove any misplaced shoots on branches. Thin the clusters of spurs if they become overcrowded. Occasionally, replace older sub-branches by cutting back to a strong shoot.

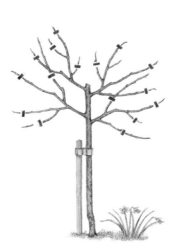

SPUR-BEARERS Continue to cut back the new growth of the main leaders by a quarter to one-third. Develop the fruiting spurs by cutting the shoots not required for branch development back to four buds. Continue to remove any crossing or misplaced shoots or branches.

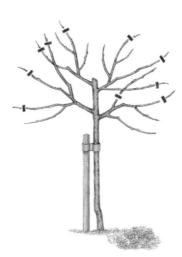

TIP-BEARERS Tip-bearing apples should only have the new growth on the main branches cut back by a quarter. Do not prune any of the other shoots unless they are crossing or misplaced, in which case they should be removed or cut back to a suitable shoot or growth bud.

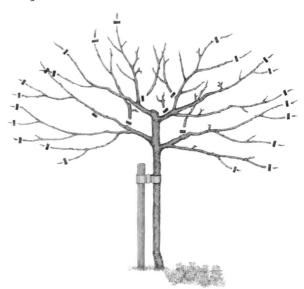

TIP-BEARERS Once tip-bearing trees have become established, little or no pruning is required. Just cut back the tips. Cut out any crossing or congested wood, especially towards the centre of the tree, which should be kept as open as possible.

Apple bush tree

Bush trees are similar in form to standards and semi-standards but are smaller. This makes them useful to anyone with a small garden. A well-developed bush is still tall enough to sit under and looks like a smaller version of a fully grown tree, which may be important for the design of the garden. Again, like standards and semi-standards, bush trees are suitable for both spur- and tip-bearing varieties.

Supports

Choose a stout stake, and insert this into the ground before the tree is planted. Avoid doing it after planting as this can damage the roots. In exposed positions, a stake on either side is more secure. Use proprietary tree ties, as these are designed to expand so that they do not rub and bruise the bark.

Initial training

You will need to start with a feathered tree, which is staked. As the young tree grows, gradually remove the lowest side branches in order to

ABOVE Bush trees are the best type of apple if you want a "tree-shaped" tree. They are relatively small, even on larger rootstock.

ABOVE There is nothing quite as rewarding as growing your own fruit. This apple will taste as good as it looks.

create a bare trunk. Do this until the trunk has reached the height you want. You should now remove the leader. The tree's main branches now develop from this point and any remaining branches on the trunk should be removed. As usual, ensure that the branches are well spread and remove any that cross. Shorten the shoots that develop on the branches so that the tree branches out. Keep the centre of the tree open.

Established pruning

You will usually only need to prune bush trees in the winter. The method you use depends on whether the tree is spur-bearing or tip-bearing. For spur-bearing apples, remove any overly vigorous and unwanted wood, as well as any branches that are crossing or rubbing. The leaders of all the branches can be reduced by about a quarter to one-third of the previous season's growth. If any of the spurs are overcrowded, then remove the older and less productive wood. For tip-bearing apples, either leave the young wood unpruned or just remove the tip back to a bud. Remember to take out older wood back to young shoots to ensure renewal and continued fruiting. As usual, take out any crossing or rubbing branches, and any that are too vigorous or misplaced. Try to keep the centre of both types reasonably open.

ABOVE An apple bush tree can make a decorative, as well as productive, feature in a domestic garden. This variety is 'Pruniflora'.

TRAINING AN APPLE BUSH TREE

Bush trees are ideal for the small garden as they do not need a great deal of training or pruning once they are established. Both initial training and the pruning are very similar to that of standard and semi-standard trees, except that the tree is on a smaller scale. Both tip- and spur-bearers are started in the same way, but from the third year onwards they are treated differently.

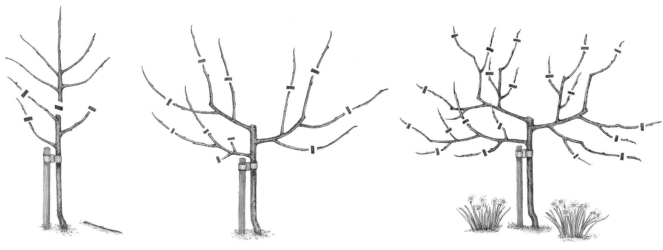

SPUR- AND TIP-BEARERS In winter, plant a young feathered tree. Grow on until the top branches have reached the required height. Remove the leader and prune back the branches so that they will divide. Remove any laterals below what will be the lowest branches.

SPUR- AND TIP-BEARERS Remove any shoots that cross over or rub, and cut back new growth on main leaders by half. Any side shoots not required as branches should also be cut back to about four buds.

SPUR-BEARERS Cut back new shoots to about five buds, once the bushes are established. Continue to remove any misplaced shoots or branches. Thin the clusters of spurs if they become overcrowded. Occasionally replace older sub-branches by cutting back to a strong shoot.

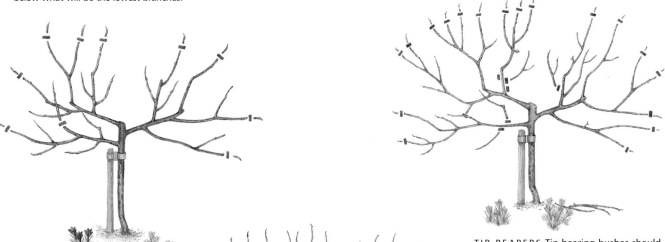

SPUR-BEARERS Continue to cut back the new growth of the main leaders by a quarter to one-third. Develop the fruiting spurs by cutting the shoots not required for branch development back to four buds. Continue to remove any crossing or misplaced shoots or branches.

TIP-BEARERS Tip-bearing bushes should only have the new growth on the main branches cut back by a quarter in their third year. Do not prune any of the other shoots, except if they are crossing or misplaced when they should be removed or cut back to a suitable shoot or growth bud.

TIP-BEARERS Once tip-bearing bush trees have become established little or no pruning is required. Just cut back the tips. Cut out any crossing or congested wood, especially towards the centre of the tree which should be kept as open as possible.

Apple spindle bush

This form of training and pruning is derived from commercial practice. It offers an effective way of producing heavy crops on small trees, but it is not the most elegant of forms for the domestic garden, and is really used only by gardeners who want to produce the maximum number of apples in a small space, without worrying too much about the tree's appearance. The basic principle involves developing horizontal branches that will produce more fruiting buds and hence a heavier crop.

Supports

A stake that is as tall as the fruit tree will eventually grow is required. It should be inserted into the ground before the tree is planted so the tree roots are not damaged when the stake is driven into the ground. Tie the tree to the stake at several points as it develops. The stake can be left in place even once the tree has reached maturity.

Initial pruning

Plant a feathered tree against the stake and cut the leader off at around 1m (3ft) from ground level. Reduce the number of laterals to three or four. The lowest should be about 60cm (2ft) from the ground. The laterals should be well spaced, both around and up the trunk. During the first summer these laterals will develop new leaders which should be gently pulled down to as near the horizontal as possible. Hold them in place by tying them to pegs in the ground or staples towards the base of the stake. Make certain that the string does not cut into the branches. As a new leader is formed tie it in to the stake and allow further well-placed laterals to develop. You can encourage this

ABOVE Spindle bushes allow a number of varieties to be grown within a small space, giving the appearance of a small orchard.

TRAINING AN APPLE SPINDLE BUSH

Spindle bush trees can look rather more complicated to train and prune than other fruit tree shapes, largely because of the strings, but, in fact, they are not at all difficult and the resulting productivity can be well worth the effort.

process by cutting back the leader each winter by about one-third to a bud on the opposite side to that from which growth emerged the year before. Allow the side branches to develop, removing any vigorous or crossing growth. Aim to keep the branches horizontal and open to the light and air. When the leader has reached the desired height of around 2–2.2m (6–7ft) (the highest that can be comfortably reached without a ladder), cut it back to two buds each year.

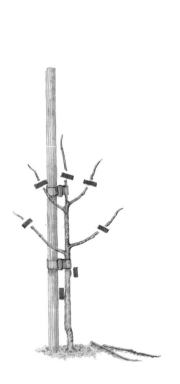

YEAR ONE, WINTER Spindle bushes are started by planting a young feathered tree. It should be secured to a strong, firm stake that is taller than the young tree. Take out the leader at about 1m (3ft) above the ground. Cut out the bottom laterals up to about 60cm (2ft).

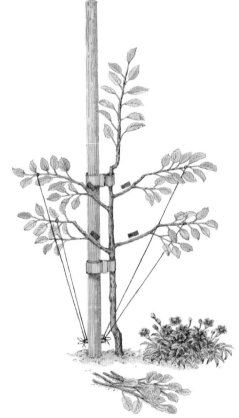

YEAR ONE, SUMMER During the tree's first summer, pull the remaining laterals gently down and tie them to staples at the bottom of the stake, or to pegs that have been inserted into the ground. Tie the new leader to the stake as it develops.

ABOVE A spindle tree coming into production. It would be better to tie the strings to pegs in the earth rather than to the trunk.

ABOVE Rows of commercially grown spindle bushes show how relatively short they are, making them easy to prune and pick.

Established pruning

Once the tree has reached its ultimate height, prune back the leader each year to one or two buds. It should be possible to remove the strings that are holding down the branches without the branches springing back up again. Any replacement branches should be tied down so that they do not follow their natural inclination to grow upwards.

Also continue to prune out any vigorous or crossing growth. Each year allow some new growth to develop to replace some of the older wood, which can then be removed.

SUBSEQUENT YEARS Repeat these two processes each year until the spindle bush reaches the height to which you want it to grow, usually around 2–2.2m (6–7ft). Cut out any shoots that attempt to grow vertically or upset the balance of the tree.

ESTABLISHED PRUNING Once the tree has reached its ultimate height, prune back the leader each year to one or two buds. Cut out some of the older wood each year to promote new, more productive wood, and remove any crossing or rubbing wood. The strings can be removed once the tree has matured.

Apple dwarf pyramid

For the gardener with a small garden who likes to grow apples on a tree, as opposed to artificial shapes such as cordons or fans, the dwarf pyramid offers the ideal solution. The trees are on a dwarfing stock, which prevents them from becoming too vigorous, and are usually restricted to a maximum height of 2m (6ft) with a spread of around 1.2m (4ft). Because of the restricted size, the range of varieties is usually confined to spur-bearing apples, but this still provides the gardener with a far wider range of varieties than is normally found in either the supermarket or at a greengrocer.

Supports

A stout pole or stake should be inserted in the ground before the tree is planted (doing it afterwards can damage the roots). The stake should protrude at least 2m (6ft) above the ground. Use proprietary tree ties, rather than string, to attach the trunk to the stake.

Initial training

The tree is trained into a cone shape with the branches getting progressively shorter towards the top of the trunk. Start with a feathered tree with well-spaced laterals. Remove any misplaced side shoots or those that point sharply upwards. Cut back each remaining lateral to about 15cm (6in) from the trunk, if possible to an outward- (not upward-) facing bud. Reduce the length of the leader to a bud about 75cm (30in) above the ground. Take out any laterals that are below about 45cm (18in) from the ground. In the summer, remove entirely any vigorous vertical growth that appears. Leave the main leader unpruned but reduce the side shoots of the main branches to about 10cm (4in). During the second winter shorten the previous season's growth of the leaders to about 20cm (8in), cutting

ABOVE Dwarf pyramids are small enough to be easily grown in large containers, which are ideal for a courtyard or patio. The pruning involved is no different from that of dwarf pyramids planted in the open ground.

TRAINING AN APPLE DWARF PYRAMID

Dwarf pyramids are some of the best shapes and size of apple tree to grow in a small domestic garden, making it possible to grow several different varieties. In general, dwarf pyramids start to produce apples very quickly.

YEAR ONE, WINTER Plant a feathered tree. Remove the leader about 75cm (30in) above ground-level. Take out any laterals below about 45cm (18in) above the ground. Cut back all other laterals to about 15cm (6in).

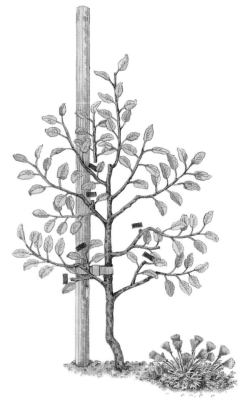

YEAR ONE, SUMMER Cut back the side shoots on the main branches in the following summer to about 10cm (4in). Leave the main leader and those of the branches unpruned.

ABOVE The central leader is cut back after planting in its first winter. It is cut back to a good bud, about 75cm (30in) above the ground.

to a downward-facing bud. The main leader should also be cut back by about two-thirds, to a bud on the opposite side to that from which growth emerged the previous year. In the second summer reduce the new growth of the main branch leaders to about 20cm (8in) and that of the side shoots to about 15cm (6in).

Established pruning

Once the tree has attained its outline, probably in its third year, it will need pruning twice a year to keep it compact. In summer, cut back the new growth of all main stems to about six leaves. Cut back all new shoots to about half this. At the same time reduce any new growth from the clusters of spurs to one

ABOVE Once established, new side shoots are cut back to one bud to help promote the growth of the spurs which produce the fruit.

leaf. In the winter, cut back new growth to one bud in order to promote new spurs. Also, cut back the main leader to one bud of its new growth. As the tree ages, thin out the older clusters of spurs as they become overcrowded.

YEAR TWO, WINTER In the following winter, reduce the new growth of all the branch leaders to about 20cm (8in). The new growth of the main leader should be cut back by about two-thirds.

YEAR TWO, SUMMER In the second summer, leave the main leader as it is, but again cut back the new growth of the branch leaders to about 20cm (8in) and that of the side shoots to about 15cm (6in).

ESTABLISHED PRUNING Once established, the apple tree bush will need pruning both in summer and again in winter, otherwise it will rapidly become overgrown. Follow the instructions in the main text above.

Apple cordons

The technique of training apples on wires as cordons allows a number of different varieties to be planted in a relatively small space. Admittedly, the quantities of fruit produced are not large, but it allows cropping over a long period, if the varieties are selected carefully. Cordons can also be very decorative. They make excellent screens and internal hedges.

Supports

Cordons can be planted against walls or fences or as free-standing screens trained against wires stretched between upright posts. The wires should be held away from walls and fences by about 10cm (4in) and should be spaced about 60cm (2ft) apart. The bottom wire should be about 30cm (12in) from the ground. Free-standing cordons can be supported on horizontal wires stretched between posts that are firmly embedded in the ground about 2–2.5m (6–8ft) apart.

Initial training

Plant a feathered whip so that the trunk is at an angle of about 45 degrees to the wires. Tie it in to a cane which has in turn been tied to the wires at the same angle. Cut back

PRUNING AN ESTABLISHED APPLE CORDON

1 Established cordon apples against a fence. They take up very little space and enable the gardener to grow several different varieties.

2 In the winter, prune back any new side shoots to one or two buds.

3 New growth on existing side shoots should also be cut back to one or two buds in the winter.

4 In summer, cut back the main leader once it has reached the top support. Do this every summer, cutting back to one or two buds.

5 In summer, you should also cut back any new shoots to two or three leaves.

6 Any new shoots on existing side shoots should be cut back to one leaf.

the laterals to about three or four buds. The following summer cut back any new laterals to four leaves and any sub-laterals to one or two leaves.

Established pruning

Continue to summer prune, reducing new growth on the sub-laterals to one leaf and any new laterals to two or three leaves. When the leader reaches the desired height cut it back

to one bud in winter or late spring. In the winter thin over-crowded clusters of spurs, taking out the older ones.

Pole or pillar apples

These are a modern innovation, and are essentially intended to be grown in containers. They are in effect vertical cordons, and should be pruned in the same way as conventional cordons.

ABOVE Well-maintained cordons bearing a good crop of apples. Cordons are an easy height for pruning and for picking fruit.

ABOVE Cordon apples in winter after they have been pruned. These have been grown in the open against a wire and pole support.

ABOVE A pole or pillar apple takes up very little space, thus allowing the gardener to grow several varieties even in a small garden. Prune as for cordons.

Multiple cordons

Cordons can be grown with two, three or more stems, either vertical or tilted at an angle of 45 degrees. Cut off the leader of a whip just below the bottom wire and allow two laterals to develop. Train these to the vertical, tying them to canes on the wires. Once established, prune as for two separate cordons. For a three- or five-stem cordon, allow three or five laterals to develop. Train the central one vertically, and the others at an angle and then vertically.

TRAINING A SINGLE CORDON

The initial training and regular established pruning of cordons is crucial. If these are neglected in any way the plant will quickly revert to a tree- or bush-like habit and outgrow its position within the design of the garden. The work required is not arduous, but it should be carried out every winter and summer.

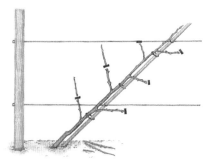

YEAR ONE, WINTER Plant a feathered whip at an angle of approximately 45 degrees. Cut back any side shoots to about three or four buds. Leave the leader uncut.

YEAR ONE, SUMMER In the first summer, cut back any new shoots on the existing side shoots to one or two leaves. Prune back any new side shoots to about four leaves.

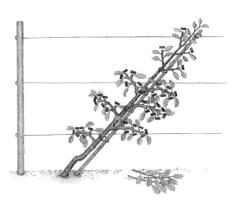

ESTABLISHED PRUNING, SUMMER Once established, the summer pruning consists of cutting back new growth on existing side shoots to one leaf and new side shoots to two or three leaves.

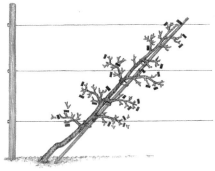

ESTABLISHED PRUNING, WINTER In winter or late spring, remove any growth on the leader to one bud. After a few years, once the clusters of spurs become congested, remove some of the older ones each year.

PRUNING MULTIPLE CORDONS

TWO-STEMMED CORDON A two-stemmed cordon with vertical stems. It is treated in exactly the same way as an ordinary cordon.

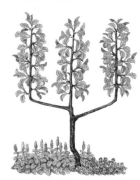

THREE-STEMMED CORDON A three-stemmed cordon in which an extra stem is grown in the middle, producing more fruit from one plant.

FOUR-STEMMED CORDON Four stemmed cordons are very decorative, but they obviously take up a lot of extra space.

ANGLED CORDON A two-stemmed cordon can be grown at 45 degrees in the same way as normal cordons.

Apple espalier

An apple espalier can be created against either a wall or fence, where it looks attractive, or free-standing against wires, to form a decorative as well as productive screen or hedge. Initially, strong supports are needed, but many established ones become totally free-standing and any support can be removed. Try to keep the shape as symmetrical as possible, with the "arms" on either side of the main stem at the same level and of the same length. This method of training is suitable only for spur-bearing apples.

Supports

Fix three (or more on a tall wall) parallel wires to a wall, fence or strong posts. The wires should be taut and between 45cm (18in) and 60cm (24in) apart. They should be held clear up to 15 cm (6in) of a wall or fence. The bottom wire should be 45–60cm (18–24in) from the ground.

Initial training

Start with either a feathered tree or a maiden whip. The former should have a good pair of opposite shoots and a strong leader or a suitable shoot

ABOVE A free-standing espalier trained against wires. Espaliers are both decorative and productive. The variety here is 'St Edmund's Pippin'.

that can be trained as a leader. The whip should be allowed to develop two strong, opposite shoots by cutting the leader back to a bud about 5cm (2in) or so above the first wire, so that new shoots will develop just beneath the wire. The first summer after planting, train what will be the horizontal shoots against canes at an angle of 45 degrees. Tie in the new

leader vertically. Cut back any other side shoots to two or three leaves. The following winter, lower the bottom branches to the horizontal. Remove any other side shoots. Also during the second winter, cut back the vertical leader to just above the second wire. Repeat the process in subsequent years until all the wires are filled. Cut back the leader.

PRUNING A YOUNG ESPALIERED APPLE

1 A young espalier showing the developing first tier and the laterals that will form the second tier, ready to be lowered into position.

2 New shoots growing on existing side shoots should be cut back to one or two buds above the base of the new wood.

3 Completely new side shoots should be cut back to three or four buds and the tip of the branch should be tied to the support.

TRAINING AN APPLE ESPALIER

It is not especially difficult to train and prune an espaliered apple, but work must be carried out regularly each winter and summer, otherwise the espalier will soon become overgrown and out of shape. The basic principles are the same as those for training a cordon, but you will be working mainly on a horizontal plane, as the espalier is trained against a wall or fence.

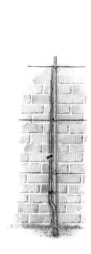

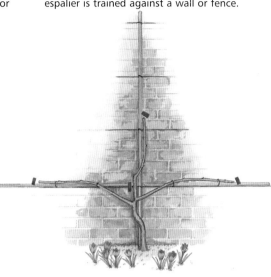

YEAR ONE, WINTER In winter plant a maiden whip against a cane that is tied to the wire supports. Cut it off just above the lower wire.

YEAR ONE, SUMMER As the two side shoots develop, tie them in to canes tied to the wires at an angle of 45 degrees. The new leader should be tied in vertically. Any other side shoots should be cut back to two or three leaves.

YEAR TWO, WINTER During the second winter, gently lower the two bottom branches to the horizontal and tie them to the wire to form the bottom tier. Cut the leader just above the second wire and remove all other side shoots.

YEAR TWO, SUMMER As the second-tier branches develop, tie them in at an angle of 45 degrees. Tie the leader to the vertical cane. Cut back the side shoots on the lower tiers to three leaves. Tie in the tips of the bottom tier as they grow.

SUBSEQUENT YEARS, SUMMER AND WINTER Continue to tie in and lower the various tiers as they develop, one level a year. Prune new shoots back to three leaves if needed; if not, cut them out. Prune new shoots on old ones back to one leaf in summer. In winter, thin the spurs if necessary.

Established pruning

Remove the canes and tie branches directly to the wires. Prune each summer, cutting back the new growth on the side shoots to one leaf, to promote the growth of fruiting spurs. Once established, remove any new growth springing directly from the main branches. In winter, thin out the clusters of spurs if necessary, cutting out the oldest and any unproductive spurs.

New shoots arising from the main trunk can be cut back initially to three leaves and then treated as a spur as on the tiers. It is important that you only allow one or two to develop between each tier.

Apple fan

Fans are an attractive way of growing apples against walls or large fences, but they do need considerable space and a strong support. Avoid excessively windy positions for free-standing fans, as they will not be stable when in full leaf.

Supports

Use five to seven parallel wires, about 30cm (12in) apart. They should be pulled taut and held 10–15cm (4–6in) away from the wall to allow air to circulate and prevent the tree from rubbing against the wall. The bottom wire should be about 45cm (18in) above ground-level. For a free-standing fan, the posts must be solidly set in the ground, 2–2.5m (6–8ft) apart.

Initial training

Buy a feathered tree that has two strong shoots just below the proposed position of the bottom wire. Cut off the leader just above the upper of these two. Tie the laterals to canes, then attach these to the wires at an angle of about 40 degrees or so. Shorten the shoots back to about 45cm (18in) to a bud on the underside. This will stimulate the production of side shoots later that year. Tie these in to new canes as they develop. The top bud will produce a new leader for each of the main arms and this should be tied in along the cane in the same direction. Cut out any unwanted shoots, aiming to keep both sides balanced. Remove any new growth from the main trunk. Cut back the tips of laterals on either side of the main stems so that they in turn branch out. Remove any growth that projects from the fan. Over the next three years or so, gradually allow the fan to develop so that it branches more towards the periphery and covers the entire space evenly.

TRAINING AN APPLE FAN

Fans, like most decorative forms of apple, need a lot of care and attention in order to prevent them from becoming overgrown and out of hand. An apple trained in this way will need attention both in the summer and in the winter.

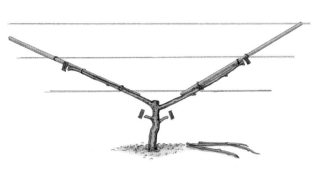

YEAR ONE, WINTER Start with a feathered tree which is planted in winter. Cut off the leader just below the bottom wire and tie in two laterals to canes attached to the wires at 40 degrees. Cut these back to about 45cm (18in). Shorten any other remaining laterals to a couple of buds.

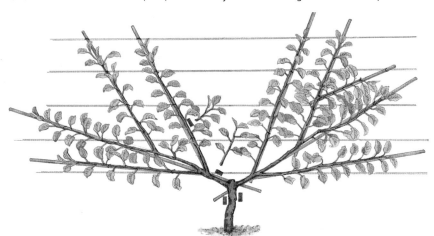

YEAR ONE, SUMMER In the following summer tie in the side shoots that develop on the laterals to form an even spread of branches, but remove any that crowd the space. Now remove any side shoots that you cut back in the winter from the main trunk.

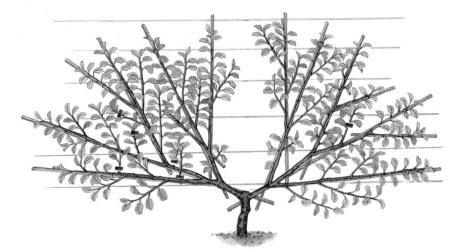

SUBSEQUENT YEARS, SUMMER Continue to tie in the developing side shoots so that a fan-like framework of branches is developed. Cut out their tips so that they continue to branch. Cut back any unwanted shoots to two or three leaves to create fruiting spurs.

Established pruning

Once the branches have matured, remove the canes and tie the stems directly to the wires. Prune each summer, cutting back the new growth on the side shoots to one leaf. Also cut out any new growth at the ends of the main branches to restrict further growth and to promote the production of fruiting spurs. Once established, remove any new growth that crowds the existing fan. In winter, thin the clusters of spurs if necessary, cutting out the oldest and any unproductive ones. Keep the fans tied back firmly to their supports because they can easily be blown away from the wall or wires, causing damage to the tree.

RIGHT Fans for growing apples are not as common as for other fruit, but nonetheless they are a valid decorative and productive way of growing them.

ESTABLISHED PRUNING, SUMMER AND WINTER In summer, reduce any new shoots on the spurs to one leaf and either cut out new shoots or reduce them to two or three leaves to create more spurs. In winter, thin out the clusters of spurs if necessary by removing the older ones.

PEARS (*Pyrus communis*)
Pear bush tree

Pears used to be grown as standard trees, which would eventually become rather large. Free-standing pear trees can still be seen in gardens, although many are now getting rather aged. Nowadays if you want to grow pears as free-standing plants, bushes are the usual form, or dwarf pyramids if you want something really small. Generally, pear trees are more upright-growing than apples, but the training and pruning are very similar.

Varieties

European Pears
'Bartlett'
'Beth'
'Beurré Hardy'
'Black Worcester'
'Comice'
'Concorde'
'Conference'
'Doyenné du Commice'
'Durondeau'
'Glou Morceau'
'Jargonelle'
'Joséphine de Malines'

'Louise Bonne of Jersey'
'Merton Pride'
'Onward'
'Ubileen'
'Williams
    Bon Chrétien'

Supports

Insert a strong stake into the ground in the planting hole before planting the tree. If you plant the tree first, it is only too easy to damage the roots, hidden by the soil, by driving the stake through them. Secure the trunk of the tree to the post with a proprietary tree tie that is designed not to rub and damage the bark.

Initial training

Start with a feathered tree, staked. As it grows, gradually remove the lowest side branches to create a bare trunk.

ABOVE An attractive group of 'Williams Bon Chrétien' pear blossoms, illustrating how they are concentrated on a cluster of spurs.

Continue to do this until the trunk has reached the required height. Now remove the leader. The main branches then develop from this point and any remaining branches on the trunk can be removed. Ensure that the branches are well spread and remove any that cross. Shorten the shoots that develop on these branches so that the tree branches out. Keep the centre of the tree open, countering the natural tendency of pears to grow upright.

PRUNING A FEATHERED PEAR BUSH

1 The young feathered pear bushes in this nursery bed are now ready for transplanting to their final positions.

2 Cut off the leader above a strong bud at the height where you want the trunk to finish, using a sloping cut away from the bud.

3 Cut out any over-strong growth that might form a new leader or unbalance the tree. Remove any laterals low down on the trunk.

4 Cut back the remaining side shoots by about half to promote a branched shape. Cut to an outward-facing bud.

TRAINING A PEAR BUSH TREE

The development of a pear bush does not differ greatly from that of a similarly shaped apple tree. Also, like the apple, once established it needs far less pruning than the more decorative forms of pear tree. Unless they are deliberately kept small, pear bush trees will usually need steps or even a ladder in order to prune them and pick the fruit.

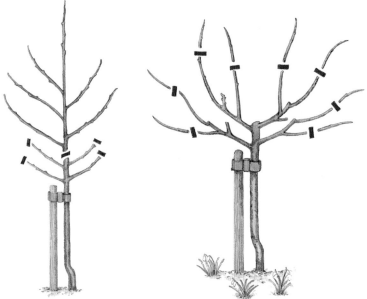

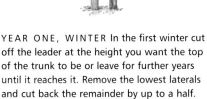

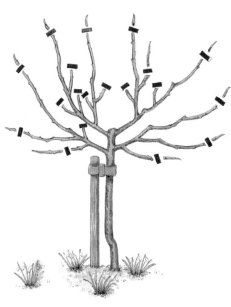

YEAR ONE, WINTER In the first winter cut off the leader at the height you want the top of the trunk to be or leave for further years until it reaches it. Remove the lowest laterals and cut back the remainder by up to a half.

YEAR TWO, WINTER In the second winter shorten the new branch leaders and side shoots to promote more branching. Remove any crossing or crowding branches, especially towards the centre which should be kept open.

SUBSEQUENT YEARS, WINTER Continue in the same fashion until the tree fills out to its final shape. Once this has been achieved there is little pruning except to thin the spurs if they become congested.

Established pruning

Generally only winter pruning is required for pear bushes. Once established, bush trees do not grow particularly vigorously and pruning is restricted mainly to thinning spurs. But you should remove any excessively vigorous and unwanted wood, along with any branches that cross or rub against each other. If the leaders are over-long reduce them by about a quarter to one-third of the previous season's growth. Check the spurs. Any that are overcrowded should have their older and less productive wood removed.

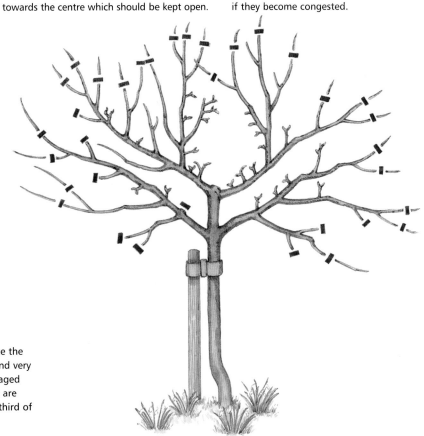

ESTABLISHED PRUNING, WINTER (*right*) Once the tree is established it requires no summer pruning and very little winter pruning. Just remove any dead or damaged wood and thin the spurs if necessary. If the leaders are over-long, reduce them by about a quarter to one-third of the previous season's growth.

Pear dwarf pyramid

Dwarf pyramids are the best tree-shaped pear trees for the small garden. They take up relatively little space and they do not require a ladder for pruning, netting or harvesting. They are excellent for mixing with dwarf pyramid apples for making a small but productive fruit garden. The basic principle is to create cone- or pyramid-shaped trees on which even the lowest branches receive plenty of air and light.

Supports
A strong pole or stake should be inserted in the planting hole first, so that the roots of the tree can be

ABOVE Mid-summer and these 'Williams Bon Chrétien' are developing well. The fruit has been thinned so that each pear has the space and supply of energy to develop fully.

spread around it before the hole is filled in (doing it afterwards can damage the roots). The stake should protrude at least 2m (6ft) above the ground. It is important to use proprietary tree ties, rather than string, to support the trunk.

Initial training
Start with a feathered tree with good, well-spaced laterals. Remove any misplaced side shoots or those that point too sharply upwards. Cut back remaining laterals to about 15cm (6in) from the trunk, if possible to an outward- (not upward-) facing bud. Reduce the length of the leader to a bud about

TRAINING A PEAR DWARF PYRAMID

Dwarf pyramids are the smallest of the tree forms of pears and are ideal for use in small gardens. However, it is important to keep them well-pruned or they will grow into rather untidy trees and eventually outgrow their space. Dwarf pyramids should normally be kept low enough so that they can be pruned and picked from the ground.

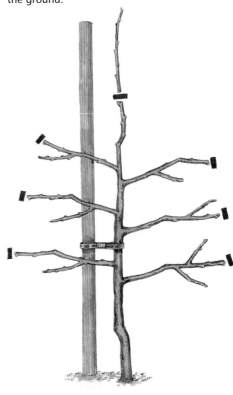

YEAR ONE, WINTER Plant a young feathered tree in winter. Cut the leader back to about 75cm (30in) from the ground. Remove the laterals below about 45cm (18in) and prune the remainder back to about 15cm (6in).

YEAR ONE, SUMMER In the following summer, remove any vigorous vertical growths (except the leader) and shorten any side shoots on the main laterals to about 10cm (4in). Leave the tips of the laterals unpruned.

YEAR TWO, WINTER In the second winter, cut back the new growth on the main laterals to about 20cm (8in), preferably to a downward-facing bud. The leader should also be reduced, cutting back the new growth by about two-thirds.

ABOVE A cluster of 'Conference' pears that are on the verge of ripening. They are best eaten straight from the tree.

75cm (30in) above the ground. Remove any laterals that are below about 45cm (18in) from the ground. In the summer, remove any vigorous vertical growths that appear. Leave the main branches unpruned but shorten the side shoots to about 10cm (4in). During the second winter, shorten the new growth of the main branches to about 20cm (8in), cutting to a downward-facing bud. The main leader should also be cut back by about two-thirds, to a bud on the opposite side to that from which growth emerged the previous year. In the second summer reduce the main branches to about 20cm (8in), and their side shoots to about 15cm (6in).

Established pruning

Once the tree has attained its outline, probably by its third year, it will need pruning twice a year to keep it compact. In summer cut back new growth on all main branches to about six leaves. Cut back all new shoots to about half this. At the same time, reduce any new growth from the clusters of spurs to one leaf. In winter, thin out the older spurs as they become crowded, and cut back the main leader to one bud of the new growth.

YEAR TWO, SUMMER During the second summer, cut back all the new growth on the lateral side shoots to about 15cm (6in). The main branches themselves should have the new growth cut back to about 20cm (8in). Leave the leader.

ESTABLISHED PRUNING, WINTER AND SUMMER Prune in winter by cutting the new growth on the main leader back to one bud, and thin the clusters of spurs if necessary. In summer, cut back new growth on main branches to about six leaves and new side shoots to three leaves. The new growth on spur clusters should be cut back to one leaf.

Pear espalier

Espaliered pears can be a very
decorative feature in the garden,
especially when mature. They look
particularly good on walls, and some
old specimens are seen on the gable
ends of houses, where they can have
five, six or even more tiers.

Supports

Attach three (or more on a tall wall)
parallel wires to a wall, fence or
strong posts. The wires should be
taut, between 45cm (18in) and
60cm (24in) apart and held at least
10cm (4in) clear of the wall. The
bottom wire should be 45–60cm
(18–24in) above the ground.

Initial training

Purchase the tree either as a feather
or a maiden whip. The former
should have a good pair of opposite
laterals and a good leader or an
upper shoot that can be trained
as a leader. The whip should be
encouraged to develop two good,

ABOVE A pear espalier growing against a fence. They can also be trained against walls or grown free-standing on a post-and-wire structure.

ABOVE An abundant crop of luscious-looking pears is the result of careful training and good pruning techniques.

opposite shoots by cutting the leader
back to a bud about 5cm (2in) or so
above the first wire, thus encouraging
new shoots to develop just beneath
the wire. Train these new shoots as
shown in the illustrations. What will
eventually be the horizontal branches
are trained at an angle of 45 degrees
against canes in their first summer,
then lowered during the second
winter to the horizontal. Remove any
other laterals. Also during the second
winter, cut back the vertical leader to
just above the second wire. Repeat
the process in subsequent years
until all the wires are filled. Cut back
the leader.

Established pruning

Remove the canes and tie the
branches directly to the wires. Prune
each summer, cutting back the new
growth on the side shoots to one
leaf, also pruning back any new
growth at the ends of the main
branches both to restrict growth
and to promote the production of

fruiting spurs. Also remove any new
growth springing directly from the
main branches. In winter, thin out
the clusters of spurs as necessary,
cutting out the oldest and less
productive ones.

ABOVE In fruitful years the pears may be produced in thick clusters and it can be an idea to thin them out when they reach this size.

TRAINING A PEAR ESPALIER

Espaliers are a tiered system of growing pears. They normally have three or four parallel branches on either side of the main trunk but they can go up to any height you like, and are sometimes trained as a decorative feature to cover the whole of the end of a house or barn, creating a splendid visual display as well as a productive tree.

YEAR ONE, WINTER In winter plant a maiden whip against a cane tied to the wire supports. Cut it off just above the lower wire, leaving two good buds to develop into the side shoots.

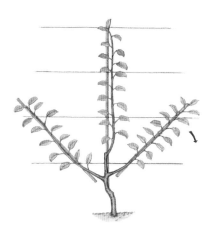

YEAR ONE, SUMMER In the first summer after planting, as the two side shoots develop, tie them in to canes tied to the wires at an angle of 45 degrees. The new leader should be tied in vertically. Any other side shoots should be cut back to two or three leaves.

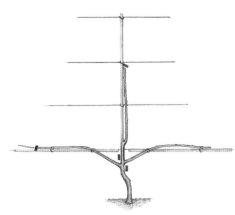

YEAR TWO, WINTER In the second winter, gently lower the two bottom branches to the horizontal and tie to the wire to form the bottom tier. Cut the leader just above the second wire and remove all other side shoots.

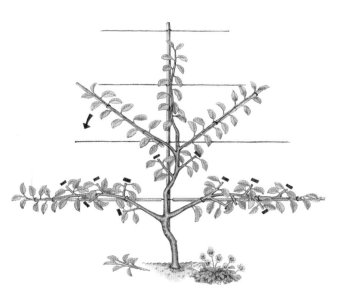

YEAR TWO, SUMMER As the second-tier branches develop, tie them in at 45 degrees. Tie the leader to the vertical cane. Cut back any side shoots on the lower tiers to three leaves. Tie in the tips of the bottom tier as it grows.

SUBSEQUENT YEARS, WINTER AND SUMMER Continue to tie in and lower the various tiers of the espalier as they develop, working on one level a year until the espalier is established. Prune new shoots back to three leaves if they are needed for the overall shape; if they are not needed, cut them out completely. Prune new shoots on old ones back to one leaf in the summer. In the winter, thin the spurs if this is necessary.

Pear fan

This is not such a popular method of training pears as an espalier, but when done well it can be an attractive way of clothing a wall or tall fence. Fan-trained pears need a lot of space to look their best. Alternatively, they can be free-standing, trained on wires.

Supports

Use five to seven parallel wires set about 30cm (12in) apart. They should be pulled taut and held at least 10cm (4in) away from the wall to allow air to circulate and prevent the tree from rubbing. The bottom wire should be about 45cm (18in) from the ground. If free-standing, the posts must be solidly set in the ground, 2–2.5m (6–8ft) apart.

Initial training

Select a young feathered tree with two strong shoots that will lie just below the position of the bottom wire. Cut off the leader just above

ABOVE A splendid free-standing pear fan, growing against a support of wires and posts. Trees trained in this way can also be grown against walls and fences.

these two laterals. Tie the laterals to canes, and tie the canes to the wires at an angle of about 40 degrees. Shorten these shoots back to about 45cm (18in) to a bud on the underside. This will stimulate new

side shoots later that year, which can also be tied in against canes as they develop. The top bud on each lateral will produce a new leader, and this should be tied in along the cane in the same direction as this main stem.

ABOVE A 'Doyenné Du Comice' pear showing how a fan is spread out to expose the fruit. Some of the older wood will need to be removed.

ABOVE A pear shoot showing the cluster of spurs that provides blossom and fruit. This has the right number of buds and is not too congested.

ABOVE Pear fans can also be trained against more permanent supports, as on this sturdy piece of trellis.

ABOVE If the pear crop is potentially heavy, it may be necessary to thin them at this stage to ensure that the rest develop properly.

TRAINING A PEAR FAN

Pears make great subjects for training as decorative fans. The process is very similar to that of apple fans; indeed, the principle behind all fans is very much the same. They will take several years to develop fully, but the result is very rewarding and well worth the effort. Unless they are enormous, most fans can be pruned and the fruit picked easily from the ground.

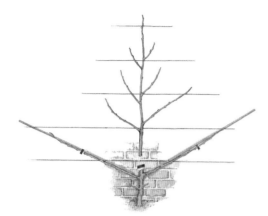

YEAR ONE, WINTER Plant the tree and cut off the leader below the bottom wire so that the top two laterals form the bottom branches. Tie these to canes at about 40 degrees and shorten to about 45cm (18in).

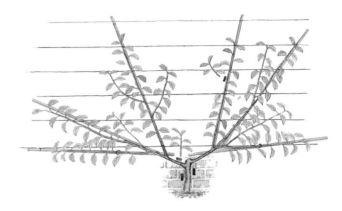

YEAR ONE, SUMMER In the first summer tie in the developing sub-laterals and the new branch leaders, creating an equal spread of branches on either side of the main trunk. Remove any unwanted young shoots from the main branches.

Cut out any unwanted shoots, aiming to keep both sides balanced. Remove any new growth from the main trunk. Cut back the tips of sub-laterals on either side of the main stems so that they in turn branch out. Remove any growth that projects out from the fan. Over the next three years or so gradually allow the fan to develop so that it branches more towards the periphery and covers the space evenly.

SUBSEQUENT YEARS (right) Continue in the same vein until all the space has been filled. Remove any shoots that stick out at the front or back and any others that cause crowding, especially in the centre of the fan. Aim to get an even coverage.

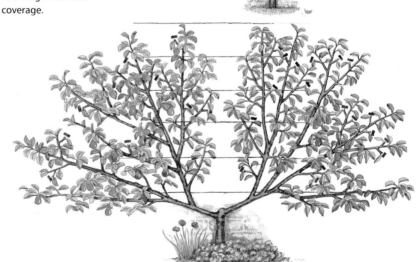

Established pruning

The fan will look better if, once the branches have matured, the canes are removed and the stems tied directly to the wires. Each summer, prune the fan by cutting back the new growth on the side shoots to one leaf, and also cutting out any new growth at the ends of the main branches, both to restrict growth and to promote the production of fruiting spurs. Once established, remove any new growth that may crowd the existing growth. In winter, thin out any congested clusters of spurs, cutting out the oldest and any unproductive ones.

ESTABLISHED PRUNING, SUMMER AND WINTER Once established, remove the canes and tie directly to the wirework. Summer prune the new growth on the side shoots back to one leaf. Cut out any new growth at the ends of the main branches. Continue to remove shoots that cause crowding or congestion. In winter thin overcrowded clusters of spurs.

PLUMS (*Prunus domestica*)
Plum bush tree

Plum bushes are the ideal size for producing large quantities of plums in the garden. They are smaller than a standard or semi-standard but are still large enough to require the use of a ladder for pruning, netting and picking. Plum pruning is mainly undertaken in mid-summer (and in early spring during the formative years). Avoid pruning in winter, as the open wounds provide an entry point for certain diseases such as silver leaf and canker.

Varieties

Dessert	Cooking
'Ariel'	'Belle de Louvain'
'Cambridge Gage'	'Czar'
'Coe's Golden Drop'	'Early Rivers'
'Early Laxton'	'Laxton's Cropper'
'Greengage'	'Pershore Yellow'
'Jefferson'	
'Kirke's Blue'	
'Marjorie's Seedling'	
'Merton Gem'	
'Oulin's Gage'	
'Victoria'	

TRAINING A PLUM BUSH

Plum bush trees are suitable for the larger garden, especially where the gardener wants to have a large crop of plums, perhaps for jam or freezing. Once trained, very little pruning is necessary to keep the trees in shape and productive. Any pruning should be restricted to the summer to avoid disease which can enter through wounds in the tree.

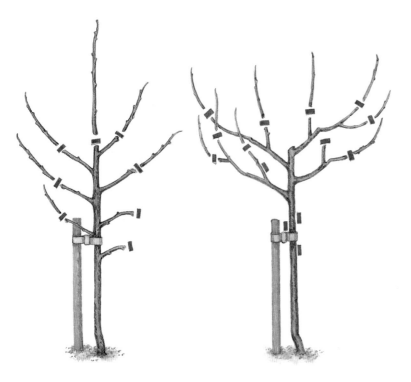

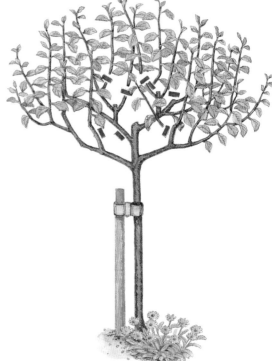

YEAR ONE, WINTER Plant a feathered tree in winter. In early spring, remove the leader at the point where you want the top branch to begin, around 1.5m (5ft) from the ground. Reduce all the remaining laterals by about two-thirds to outward-facing buds.

YEAR TWO, SPRING In the following spring, select four or so of the top laterals to become the main branches and remove all the others completely. Remove any shoots from the main branches that are misplaced or causing crowding. Cut back the new growth on the main branches and their shoots by about half to two-thirds to outward-facing buds.

ESTABLISHED PRUNING, SUMMER Once established, only prune in mid-summer. This is restricted to removing dead or damaged wood and taking out any crossing or congested branches. Also cut out any vigorous vertical growths that appear anywhere on the tree.

ABOVE Clusters of ripening plums. One or more of these could have been removed at an earlier stage to allow the others to fill out more.

Supports

Knock a short stake into the planting hole and spread out the roots. Do not plant the tree and then put in the stake as you may damage the roots beneath the soil. Use a proprietary tree tie to connect the two. In windy areas use two stakes, one on each side of the tree.

Initial pruning

Buy a feathered tree and plant it against a stake. In early spring, shorten the leader at about 1.5m (5ft) from the ground, immediately above a bud, which will produce the top branch. Reduce all laterals by about two-thirds, to outward-facing buds. The following spring, remove all laterals up to about 60cm (2ft) above the ground to produce a tree with a clear trunk. Also, either remove any branches that are misplaced, crowded or crossing other branches completely or cut them back to a bud that will produce a better-placed replacement branch. Remove any shoots from the main branches that are misplaced or causing crowding, especially towards the centre of the tree. Cut back the tips of all remaining shoots by half to two-thirds, to outward-facing buds.

Established pruning

By the third year, the plum bush tree should have achieved its mature size. From now on, prune only in mid-

ABOVE Trees with heavy crops may need their branches to be propped up with poles to prevent them breaking.

summer. In fact, there is not a great deal of pruning to be done except to remove dead, diseased or damaged wood, as usual, along with any weak or crossing wood. You should also remove any upright growths (suckers) that appear on the main or subsidiary branches.

ABOVE Greengages are another type of plum and are treated, as far as the pruning is concerned, in exactly the same way as a plum.

ABOVE A good crop of damsons in late summer. Damsons and bullaces are best grown as bush trees and pruned in the same manner as other plums.

Plum pyramid

For the small garden, a pyramid is the ideal way of growing plums. A pyramid is a short, conical tree on which the branches decrease in size as they progress up the tree. The pyramid shape ensures that even the lower branches receive plenty of light with good air circulation. The short stature also makes a plum pyramid easy to prune, net and pick, while providing a reasonable crop of fruit.

Supports

A single stake should be placed in the ground before the tree is planted. Putting the stake in after the tree may result in the roots hidden beneath the surface being damaged. Use a proprietary tree tie to attach the trunk to the stake.

Once the tree has become established, the stake can be removed except in very exposed positions. Regularly check that the tie is not too tight and cutting into the growing trunk.

Initial training

Choose a feathered tree and plant it in the winter. In early spring, remove all laterals up to about 45cm (18in) from the ground. Cut out the tip of the leader at a height of about 1.5m (5ft). Reduce the remaining laterals by about half, cutting to an outward-facing bud. In the following mid-summer, cut back all sub-laterals to about 15cm (6in) and take back the new growth of the main branch stems to about 20cm (8in), cutting to an outward-facing bud. In the following early spring, cut back the previous year's growth on the main leader by about two-thirds.

Established pruning

Once the tree is mature, prune only in summer to avoid diseases such as

ABOVE 'Victoria' plums are one of the most popular varieties. They can produce heavy crops which may mean the branches require props.

ABOVE A lovely crop of succulent plums are the reward of well-tended trees. Compact trees will make these easy to harvest from the ground.

TRAINING A PLUM DWARF PYRAMID

Some varieties of plum lend themselves to being grown on a dwarfing stock and can be grown as dwarf pyramids. Check that you buy a suitable variety. These are particularly useful in a small garden where just a small quantity of plums is required. Because of their small size it may be possible to grow several varieties of plum as pyramids in a small area.

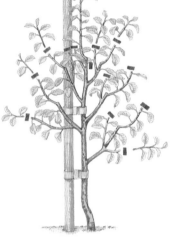
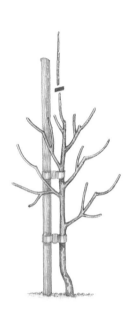

YEAR ONE, WINTER
Plant a feathered tree in winter. In early spring, cut out its leader at about 1.5m (5ft) from the ground. Cut out all the side shoots below about 45cm (18in) and then reduce all remaining laterals by about half.

YEAR ONE, SUMMER The following mid-summer you will need cut back the new growth on the main branches to about 20cm (8in) to an outward-facing bud. You should also cut back all the sub-laterals to around 15cm (6in).

YEAR TWO, SPRING
In the second spring cut back the new growth made by the leader by about two-thirds. No other pruning is required at this time of the year.

ESTABLISHED PRUNING, SUMMER The tree may be mature by the third spring or it may need another year. Once mature little pruning is required unless there is vigorous growth. This should be cut back to a few leaves in summer. You may also need to remove any dead, diseased or damaged wood and thin out any congested areas by taking out older wood.

silver leaf. The main pruning can be restricted to removing any dead, diseased or damaged wood and thinning any congested areas by taking out the older wood. If the tree is reasonably vigorous, you may still need to reduce the new growth on all the main branches to 20cm (8in) and on the side branches to 15cm (6in). Once the main leader has reached its ultimate height, it should be cut back to one bud of the previous year's growth in late spring.

LEFT A good crop of 'Opal' plums. In early summer, the plums have been thinned so that those remaining have space and sufficient energy to develop fully.

Plum spindle bush

While pyramids are probably the best form of plum tree for the small garden, if you are keen to get maximum cropping from your trees it is possibly a good idea to follow the trend in commercial growing, which concentrates on spindle bushes. If you already grow apples by this method you will be well aware of the technique as it is essentially the same. The idea is to keep the branches as near to the horizontal as possible.

Supports

A permanent stake that is as tall as the tree will grow is required. Insert it before planting the tree so that the roots are not damaged as you drive it into the ground. The tree can be tied to it in several places as it develops, and the stake can be left in place even after the tree matures.

ABOVE Spindle bushes are relatively small and allow a number of different varieties to be grown in a small garden. It is advisable to check with your supplier as to which varieties are suitable for training in this way.

ABOVE 'Victoria' plums are a very popular variety. The luscious fruit on this tree is the result of attentive pruning.

ABOVE A fine crop of damsons. These are pruned in exactly the same way as plums. Some have a tendency to produce suckers, which should be removed.

TRAINING A PLUM SPINDLE BUSH

A spindle bush creates a good open tree, which allows the sun to enter and ripen the fruit. Spindle bushes are no more difficult to train than any other plum trees, although the tethering strings can make them look tricky. As with all plums, it is advisable to keep the majority of pruning to mid-summer if possible.

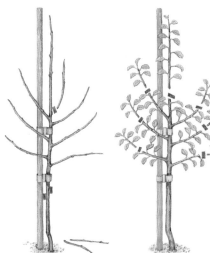

YEAR ONE, WINTER Plant a young feathered tree in winter. In early spring, remove the laterals below about 60cm (2ft), as well as any that are misplaced or at too steep an angle. Leave the rest intact.

YEAR ONE, SUMMER In mid-summer, you will need to remove the leader at about 1m (3ft) above ground-level and reduce all the laterals to about half their length.

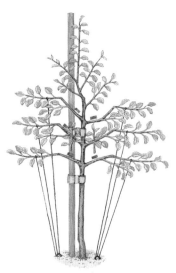

SUBSEQUENT YEARS, SUMMER As the branches develop, gradually pull them down to the horizontal using strings tied to pegs. Remove any vigorous vertical growth. As the new main leader develops, tie it in to the stake. Allow other well-placed laterals to develop. From now on, prune only in mid-summer, allowing the side branches to develop and removing any vigorous or crossing growth.

ESTABLISHED PRUNING Once the bush is established, cut back the leader to two buds each summer. Cut out any vigorous growth and any crowding laterals, but tie down any new growth that makes a useful lateral.

Initial pruning

In the winter, plant a feathered tree against a stake. The following early spring, remove completely all laterals below about 60cm (2ft) above ground-level. Leave the remainder of the laterals, including the leader, except for any that are at too sharp an angle to the trunk or that are misplaced, causing crowding or crossing. In mid-summer cut the leader off at around 1m (3ft) and reduce the length of the laterals by about half. As the new branch leaders develop, gently pull the stems down as close to the horizontal as possible, holding them in position by tying them down to pegs in the ground or hooks towards the base of the stake. Make sure that the string does not cut into the bark. Remove any vigorous growth from the laterals. As a new main leader is formed, tie it in to the stake and allow further well-placed laterals to develop. From now on only prune in mid-summer. Allow the side branches to develop, removing any vigorous or crossing growth. Aim to keep the branches horizontal and open to the light and air.

Established pruning

All pruning of established bushes should be done around mid-summer to avoid fungal diseases such as silver leaf. When the leader has reached the desired height of around 2–2.2m (6–7ft) – the highest that can be comfortably reached without a ladder – cut it back to two buds each year. Once the main branches are established in a horizontal position and no longer spring back, the strings can be removed. Continue to tie down any new growth that follows its natural tendency to grow upwards. Also continue to prune out any vigorous or crossing growth. Each year allow some new growth to develop on the spindle bush in order to replace some of the older wood, which should be removed.

Plum fan

Fans take up a lot of space and
not everybody has a wall or fence
large enough to accommodate one,
but if you do it is a very decorative
way of growing plums as well as
a good method of lessening the
effects of frost on blossom. Fans
can also be grown free-standing
against posts and wires, but need
a sheltered position.

Supports

Attach five to seven parallel wires set
about 30cm (12in) apart to a wall
or fence. They should be pulled taut
and held at least 10cm (4in) or
more away from the wall to allow
air to circulate and prevent the tree
from rubbing. The bottom wire
should be about 45cm (18in) from
the ground. If free-standing, the
posts must be solidly set in the
ground, 2–2.5m (6–8ft) apart.

Initial training

Start with a young feathered tree
that has two suitable laterals just
below the level of the first wire. In
spring, cut the leader off just above
the upper of the desired laterals.
Cut back the two laterals to about
45cm (18in) from the base to an
underside bud. Tie these laterals to
individual long canes, which you
fasten in turn to the wires at an
angle of about 40 degrees. Shorten
any other laterals to about two buds
until the summer, then cut them
off completely, tight to the trunk.
Around mid-summer, tie in the
new branch leaders to the canes.
Select the best-placed side shoots
and tie these in to the wires. Remove
the rest, especially any vigorous
vertical shoots. Try to encourage
growth downward to fill the fan
evenly. Continue to do this every
summer until the fan framework has
filled out.

ABOVE A plum fan trained against a wall, which helps to provide protection for the blossom
against destructive winter frosts.

Established pruning

Every mid-summer, cut out any dead,
diseased or damaged wood. You will
also need to remove any vigorous
growth along with any shoots that
tend to crowd the framework, and
any that point towards the wall or
outward away from the plane of the
fan. Leaders on all the branches and
side shoots should be cut back to
just a few leaves. In the spring (and
not winter), it is important to thin
out any new growth by pinching it
back, retaining only those shoots
that are required as replacements or
to fill gaps.

LEFT This cluster of
plums might have
benefited from
being thinned in the
early summer, so
that the remaining
fruit grew larger.

TRAINING A PLUM FAN

Fans are probably the most complicated way of training plums. However, the result is a very decorative bush which produces fruit well. It should preferably be trained against a wall, but fences or free-standing post-and-wire structures are also suitable. Choose a tree that has two suitable laterals just below the level of the lowest wire.

In general, fan-trained plum trees are relatively short and so they can easily be pruned and picked without the need for ladders.

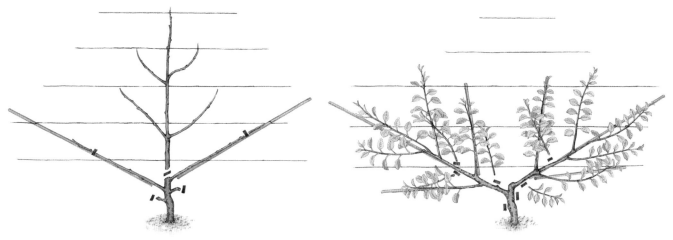

YEAR ONE, WINTER Plant a feathered tree in winter. In spring, cut off the leader just below the bottom wire. Cut back the two laterals to about 45cm (18in) and tie them to canes at about 40 degrees. Reduce the length of any other laterals to a few buds.

YEAR ONE, SUMMER In mid-summer tie in the main side shoots to canes as they develop, creating an even spread on both sides of the trunk. Select the best-placed side shoots and tie these in to the wires. Cut out any that cross or are badly placed. Continue this process every summer until the fan framework has filled out. Remove completely the remains of the cut-back laterals on the trunk.

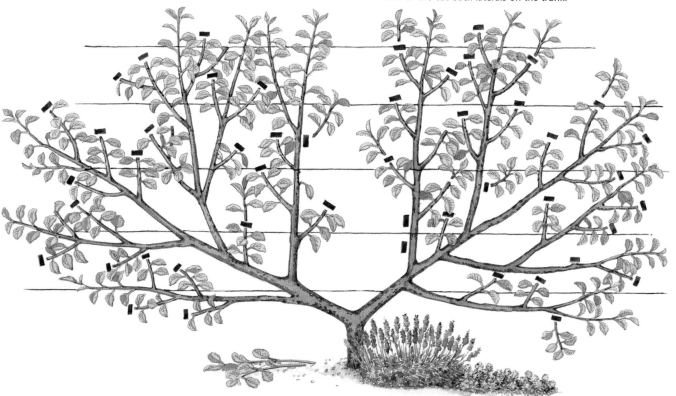

SUBSEQUENT YEARS As the fan becomes established, cut back the new growth of the main and side shoots to just two or three leaves in mid-summer. Remove completely any congested side shoots, keeping the shape relatively open so that sun reaches all the fruit. In spring, thin out any new growth, only retaining those shoots needed as replacements or to fill gaps.

CHERRIES (*Prunus* species)
Sweet cherry bush

Cherries have always been difficult for the home grower because until relatively recently there was no dwarfing stock, so the trees were too large for the average garden. The size not only made cherry trees difficult to prune and pick, but also to net, so that the birds got most of the fruit. Dwarfing stock has become easier to find, making it possible to grow dwarf bushes that are much more manageable. On the other hand, it is still possible to grow cherries as larger bushes or even as semi-standards although these are generally too large for small or even medium-size gardens. Another problem has been eased in that there are now more self-fertile varieties available. The basic pruning for the dwarf trees is the same as for the bushes given below. Cherries should only be pruned in the spring or early summer.

Varieties		
Sweet		**Acid**
'Bradbourne Black'	'Merton Biggarreau'	'Kentish Red'
'Colney'	'Merton Favourite'	'May Duke'
'Early Rivers'	'Merton Glory'	'Montmorency'
'Governor Wood'	'Napoleon	'Morello'
'Greenstem Black'	Biggarreau'	'Nabella'
'Kent Biggarreau'	'Noir de Guben'	'Reine Hortense'
'Kentish Red'	'Stella'	'The Flemish'
'Lapins'	'Sunburst'	'Wye Morello'
	'Waterloo'	

Supports

Hammer a short stake into the hole where the tree will be planted, and spread the roots around it. Avoid planting the tree and then putting in the stake, as this might damage the roots underneath the ground. It is best to use a proprietary tree tie to connect the stake and trunk. In windy areas use two stakes, one on each side of the tree.

Initial pruning

Start with a feathered tree, staked. In early spring, cut back the leader at about 1.5m (5ft) from the ground, immediately above a bud which will produce the top branch. Reduce all laterals by about two-thirds to outward-facing buds. The next spring remove all laterals up to about 1m (3ft) from the ground, to produce a tree with a clear trunk. Also prune any branches that are misplaced, crowding or crossing others, either removing them completely or cutting them back to a bud which will make a better replacement. Also remove any shoots from the main branches that are misplaced or causing crowding, especially towards the centre of the tree. Cut back the tips of all remaining shoots by a half to two-thirds to outward-facing buds.

Established pruning

By the third year, the tree should have achieved its mature size. From now on prune only in early summer. Sweet cherries mainly flower on spurs on the older wood, so pruning chiefly consists of maintaining an open habit. In fact there is not a great deal to be done except to remove dead, diseased or damaged wood along with any weak or crossing stems. Also remove any upright growths (suckers) that appear on the main or subsidiary branches. Occasionally you may need to cut back main branches to keep the cherry within its allotted space. In this case, take them back to the first established side shoot.

ABOVE Hanging bunches of cherries are easy to harvest. Acid cherries such as these are best used for cooking purposes. You could use them to make jams or bottle them.

ABOVE A good crop of 'Lapins' cherries. It is advisable to pick cherries in the early morning before the heat of the day makes the leaves droop and hide them.

TRAINING A SWEET CHERRY BUSH

It is advisable to buy cherry trees on a rootstock that is suitable for growing as bushes: those that are grown as standards and semi-standards are generally too large for the average domestic garden and it is difficult to contain their size. Choose a feathered bush with strong laterals that spread out to cover an area of between 1.2–1.5m (4–5ft).

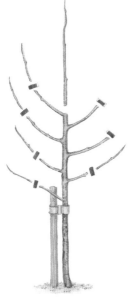
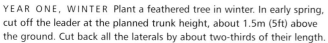

YEAR ONE, WINTER Plant a feathered tree in winter. In early spring, cut off the leader at the planned trunk height, about 1.5m (5ft) above the ground. Cut back all the laterals by about two-thirds of their length.

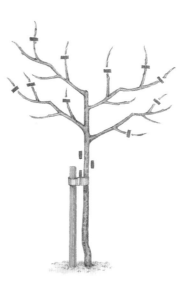

YEAR TWO, SPRING A year later, remove all laterals up to what will be the bottom branch, about 1m (3ft) from the ground. Cut out all misplaced shoots and reduce the rest by about half to two-thirds.

SUBSEQUENT YEARS Repeat until the tree has acquired its final shape and size. Future pruning should be done in early summer and only consists of removing any misplaced or over-vigorous wood.

ABOVE During the second year of training, cut back all shoots in the early part of the summer by half to two-thirds.

Sweet cherry fan

If you do not have enough room for cherry trees, you may nevertheless be lucky enough to have a wall or fence large enough to carry a fan. Although it needs a lot more pruning to keep it under control, it does have certain advantages over a tree. In particular, no ladder is necessary for pruning, picking or, very importantly, netting against birds.

Supports

If you have space on a wall or fence, attach five to seven parallel wires set about 30cm (12in) apart. Make certain that they are held at least 10cm (4in) or more away from the wall, to allow air to circulate and prevent the tree from rubbing. The bottom wire should be about 45cm (18in) from the ground. Alternatively, use free-standing posts, which must be solidly set in the ground, 2–2.5m (6–8ft) apart.

Initial training

Buy a young feathered tree that has two suitable laterals just below the level of the first wire. Plant in winter. The following spring, cut off the leader just above the upper of the desired laterals. Tie these laterals to individual long canes, and fasten the canes to the wires at an angle of about 40 degrees. Cut back the two laterals to about 45cm (18in) from the base to an underside bud. Shorten any other laterals to two buds, then cut them off completely in summer, tight to the trunk. Around mid-summer, tie in the new branch leaders to the canes. Select the best-placed side shoots and tie these into the wires. Cut out the remainder, along with any vigorous vertical shoots. Try to encourage downward growth that will fill in the fan. Continue to do this every summer until the fan has filled out.

ABOVE A sweet cherry fan in winter, clearly showing the structure of the tree. This cherry fan has been grown against a sunny fence, but it is also possible to grow the fan against a wall or in the open using a pole-and-wire structure.

Established pruning

In early summer, cut out any dead, diseased or damaged wood. Also remove any vigorous growth along with any shoots that tend to crowd the framework, and any which point towards the wall or outwards away from the plane of the fan. Leaders on all the branches and side shoots should be cut back to just a few leaves. In spring (not winter), thin out any new growth by pinching it back, retaining only those shoots that are required as replacements or

ABOVE A sweet cherry fan in summer, clearly showing the netting covering the tree. This is very important as it keeps the birds from eating all the fruit.

ABOVE A cherry fan demonstrating an even spread of blossom. This is what one should aim for when pruning.

to fill gaps. If a main lateral needs replacing, choose a suitably placed stem, tie it to a cane and then cut back the old branch. Try to keep the general shape of the fan as open as possible, while ensuring complete coverage of the space.

TRAINING A SWEET CHERRY FAN

Cherry fans should be started from feathered trees that have two good laterals which will eventually form the main branches from which the rest of the fan grows. Apart from the various stages of formative pruning, all pruning of cherries should take place in early summer to avoid disease entering winter wounds.

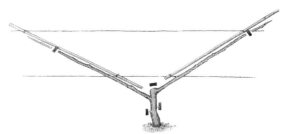

YEAR ONE, WINTER Plant a feathered tree in winter. In spring remove the leader just below the bottom wire. Tie in the two laterals to canes at about 40 degrees and then cut them back to about 45cm (18in). Shorten any laterals to two buds.

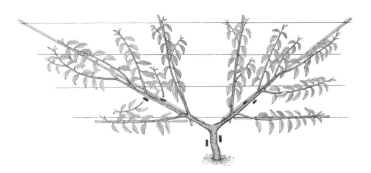

YEAR ONE, SUMMER In early to mid-summer, tie in the branch leaders to canes and the best-placed new side shoots to the wires, and cut out the rest. Cut off the laterals on the trunk completely.

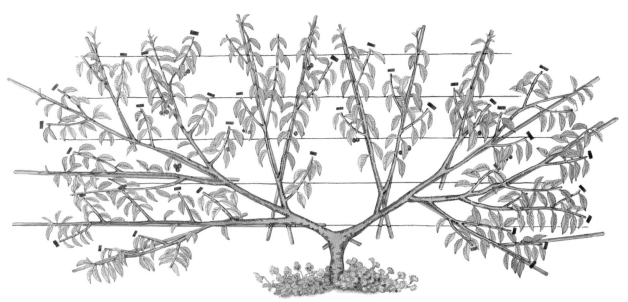

SUBSEQUENT YEARS Continue the process until the space is evenly covered with branches. Little pruning is required but, if necessary, cut out misplaced or over-vigorous shoots in early summer. Pinch back any new growth that is not required to fill a space.

PEACHES AND NECTARINES
(*Prunus persica* and *P. p.* var. *nectarina*)
Peach and nectarine bush

More and more gardeners are growing peaches and nectarines successfully in the open. The results are certainly rewarding. In cooler climates, where they will not fruit successfully as free-standing trees, fans are best, as they can be grown against protecting walls. There is no dwarfing stock as yet, but there is rootstock available that enables them to be grown successfully as bush trees.

Support
Put a stake in the ground before planting the tree so that you do not accidentally damage its roots. Use a proprietary tree tie to attach the tree to the stake, as alternatives can damage the bark.

Initial training
Plant a grafted feathered whip in winter. In the following early spring set about its formative pruning by

ABOVE Peach bushes are suitable for larger gardens, particularly in warmer areas. For small or cooler gardens the peach fan is probably better.

ABOVE A bed of young feathered peach trees just coming into bud. They can be purchased as bare-rooted specimens from nursery beds.

clearing the trunk of all laterals to about 1m (3ft) from ground-level. Select four or five well-placed laterals to form the main branches, then cut them back to about one-third of their original length. Cut back the main leader just above the top lateral. In summer, remove any new laterals that form on the trunk, unless they enhance the overall shape. The centre should be kept open, so remove any sub-laterals that tend to fill it, along with any others that are crowding or crossing other branches and shoots. The following spring, reduce all the shoot leaders by about half, cutting back to an outward-facing bud.

Varieties

Peaches	Nectarines
'Amsden June'	'Early Rivers'
'Bellegarde'	'Independence'
'Duke of York'	'John Rivers'
'Dymond'	'Lord Napier'
'Peregrine'	'Pineapple'
'Rochester'	
'Redhaven'	
'Royal George'	

nectarines

peaches

TRAINING A PEACH OR NECTARINE BUSH

Peaches are usually purchased as feathered trees. Select one with strong laterals around the area where you want the branches to be formed. As with other members of the *Prunus* genus, such as plums and cherries, established pruning tasks are best carried out in summer to avoid disease which can enter through wounds in the tree.

YEAR ONE, WINTER Plant a feathered whip in winter. In early spring clear the bottom part of the trunk of laterals. Select four or five strong laterals to form the branches and then remove the leader just above the top one. Cut these laterals back by about two-thirds.

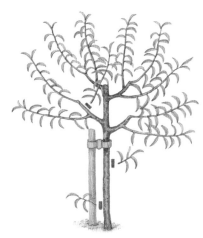

YEAR ONE, SUMMER During the following summer remove any misplaced or over-crowding shoots, making certain that the centre of the bush is kept relatively open.

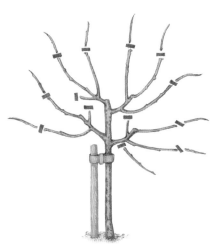

YEAR TWO, SPRING In the following spring remove all unwanted and misplaced shoots and cut back the remaining shoots by about half, to a strong bud.

Established pruning

From now on all pruning should take place in early summer. First remove any dead or damaged wood, and any shoots that are crossing or crowding other growth, especially towards the centre, which should be kept open. Fruits are produced on the previous year's wood, so remove some of the previous year's fruiting wood, preferably back to a point where there is new growth. Take out any shoots that appear on the main trunk below the bottom branch.

ABOVE There is nothing quite like eating a peach or nectarine fresh from the tree. This peach variety is called 'Redhaven'.

ESTABLISHED PRUNING Once established, as well as removing any misplaced or unwanted shoots, take out a large proportion of the wood that has fruited back to a new shoot.

Peach and nectarine fan

In many ways it is better to grow a peach or nectarine as a fan in cooler climates, provided you have a suitable wall or fence. It makes it easier to attend to the tree and to protect it against frosts and wet weather, by fixing what are in effect roller blinds of clear plastic which hang down from a frame over the plant. The wall also offers added warmth. Besides, fans always look especially attractive.

Supports

Attach parallel horizontal wires to the wall about 30cm (12in) apart, the bottom one about 45cm (18in) above the ground. The wires should be stretched taut and held about 10–15cm (4–6in) away from the wall. In warmer areas the fan can be supported on wires strung between strong posts, solidly set in the ground about 2–2.5m (6–8ft) apart.

Initial training

Start with a young feathered tree that has two suitable laterals just

ABOVE One advantage of peach and nectarine fans is that they are easier to protect from frosts than more conventional bush trees.

TRAINING A PEACH OR NECTARINE FAN

Fans are probably the best way of growing peaches and nectarines, especially if they are grown against a wall which helps keep the frosts away from the blossom. Fans are easier to reach when you are pruning and picking. They are also more decorative than conventional trees, especially if more than one is grown against a wall.

YEAR ONE, WINTER Plant a feathered tree in winter and then in spring cut back the leader to two strong laterals below the bottom wire. Tie these in to canes at 40 degrees and cut them back to about 45cm (18in). Cut back any other laterals to a few buds.

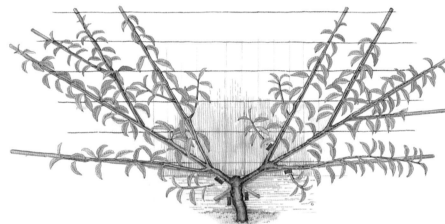

YEAR ONE, SUMMER Tie in the new branch leaders to canes and all the best-placed side shoots that you need to create an even spread to wires. Cut out any that are not needed or that are misplaced. Also remove the remains of the other laterals on the trunk.

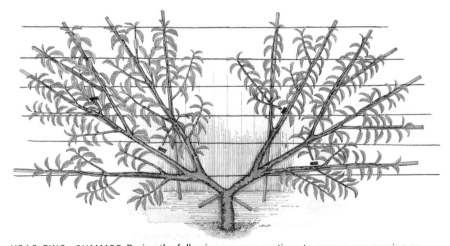

YEAR TWO, SUMMER During the following summer continue to remove any crossing or misplaced shoots, trying to ensure an even and balanced coverage on both sides of the trunk. Prevent the centre from becoming crowded.

PRUNING A PEACH FAN

1 In summer it can be an advantage to remove some of the shoots bearing leaves that shade the fruit, preventing them from ripening.

2 Some of the long shoots not bearing fruit can be cut back to one or two leaves of the new growth, opening up the fruit below.

3 The shade can be further reduced by taking out the tips of fruiting shoots. After fruiting, these will be cut back further.

below the level of the first wire. In spring, cut the leader back just above the uppermost of the desired laterals. Cut back the two laterals to about 45cm (18in) from the base to an underside bud. Tie these laterals to individual long canes, and fasten these in turn to the wires at an angle of about 40 degrees. Cut back any other laterals to two buds. In summer, cut them back completely, tight to the trunk. Around mid-summer, tie in the new branch leaders to the canes. Select the best-placed side shoots and tie these in to the wires. Remove the rest, especially vigorous, vertical shoots. Try to encourage downward growth that will fill the fan evenly. Do this each summer, tying the main shoots to canes until the fan has filled out.

Established pruning

Prune in mid-summer. Cut out any dead, diseased or damaged wood along with any vigorous growth, or stems that tend to crowd the framework and shoots which point towards the wall or project away from the plane of the fan. In late summer, after fruiting, cut back the wood that has carried fruit to a replacement shoot. Any older wood that is less productive can also be cut back to replacement shoots, which should be trained in to replace it.

ABOVE A peach fan grown against a wall. Note how easy it is for netting to be draped over the fan to protect the fruit from marauding birds.

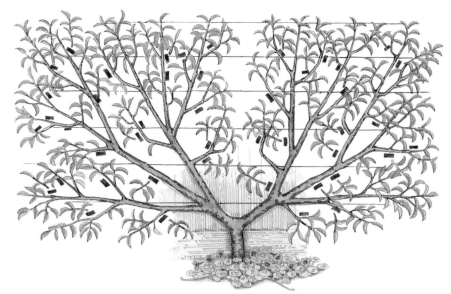

ESTABLISHED PRUNING, SUMMER Once established, cut back fruited shoots to a new shoot after fruiting. Also remove any crowding or misplaced shoots. After a few years remove the occasional old branch back to a replacement shoot.

APRICOTS *(Prunus armenica)*
Apricot fan

Apricots can be grown as bush trees, but these do not do very well in cooler climates. Grown against a wall, where they can be given winter protection, they are more successful. They can also be grown against fences, but walls provide better shelter. Glasshouses built against a wall are the ideal situation.

Supports

Fix parallel horizontal wires to the wall, spaced at about 30cm (12in) intervals, the bottom wire about 45cm (18in) above ground-level. The wires should be stretched taut and held about 10–15cm (4–6in) away from the wall. In warmer areas, the fan can be supported by a strong fence or on wires strung between sturdy posts, solidly set in the ground about 2–2.5m (6–8ft) apart.

Initial training

Start with a young feathered tree with two suitable laterals just below

Varieties

'Alfred'	'Luizet'
'Bergeron'	'Moorpark'
'Breda'	'New Large Early'
'Early Moorpark'	'Polonais'
'Hemskerk'	

the level of the first wire. The first spring after planting, cut the leader back just above the uppermost of the desired laterals. Tie them to individual long canes, and secure these to the wires at an angle of about 40 degrees. Cut back these two laterals to about 45cm (18in) from the base to an underside bud. Cut back any other laterals to two buds. In summer, cut them back completely, tight to the trunk. Around mid-summer, tie in the new branch leaders to the canes. Select the best-placed side shoots and tie these in to the wires. Remove the rest, especially any vigorous, vertical shoots. Try to encourage downward

ABOVE LEFT An apricot trained against a wall, showing the even spread of blossom over the whole fan. The wall will help to protect the blossom from frost.

LEFT A well-spread apricot fan on a wall. The two sides are slightly unbalanced but this will rectify itself as the left side catches up and some of the wayward shoots on the right are removed.

TRAINING AN APRICOT FAN

The only really successful way to grow apricots in cooler climates is with the protection of a wall, and the fan shape is the only practical way in which to do this. As with plums and cherries, the best time for pruning in order to prevent disease entering the wood is in the summer. A well-established apricot fan also has many decorative qualities.

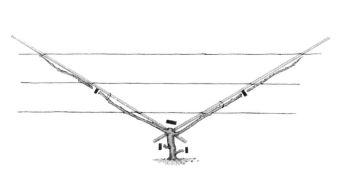

YEAR ONE, WINTER Plant a feathered tree in winter, and in spring remove the leader just below the bottom wire. Tie in two strong laterals to canes at 40 degrees and reduce their length to 45cm (18in). Cut back any other laterals to two buds.

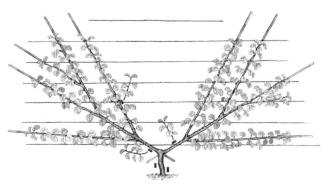

YEAR ONE, SUMMER Tie in the main side shoots as they develop, creating an even coverage of the wall and ensuring that the sides are balanced. Remove any unnecessary shoots, including the laterals on the trunk.

growth to fill the fan evenly. Do this every summer, tying the main shoots to canes, until the fan has filled out.

Established pruning

Once the fan is established, prune it in early to mid-summer only. Spring pruning can result in diseases entering the tree through the pruning wounds. Cut out any dead, diseased or damaged wood. At the same time, remove any vigorous growth, stems that tend to crowd the framework and shoots that point towards the wall or project away from the plane of the fan. New growth on all branch leaders and side shoots should be cut back to just a few leaves. Thin out any other new growth, retaining only those shoots that are required to fill gaps or to replace older stems. Periodically remove any old growth that is unproductive, cutting it back to a replacement shoot. Try to keep the centre reasonably open and clear of shoots. The canes can be removed and the shoots tied directly to the wires once the fan has reached maturity.

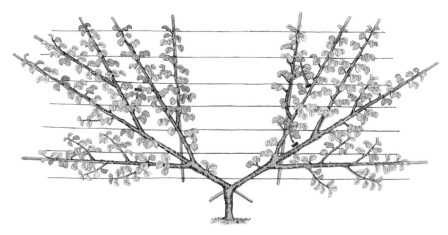

YEAR TWO, SUMMER During the following summer remove completely any vigorous vertical shoots and any misplaced ones, and tie in the rest to suitable spaces to ensure a good coverage.

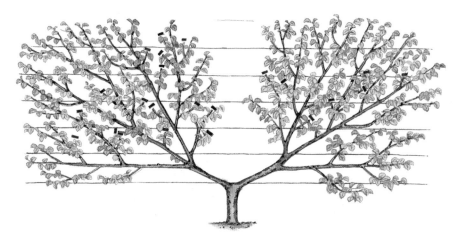

ESTABLISHED PRUNING, SUMMER Once established, continue to cut out any vigorous vertical growth and any unwanted shoots in summer. Cut back any new growth on branch leaders and all side shoots to one or two leaves. You can remove the canes when the fan is mature.

QUINCES *(Cydonia oblonica)*
Quince bush

Quinces are not grown as widely as they should be. Admittedly, the fruit cannot be eaten directly off the tree, but it is most delicious when cooked. Quinces can be grown as fans, but are best grown in the open as trees. They are also successful as multi-stemmed trees if they are kept well pruned, but bush trees are easier to maintain and produce a more reliable crop.

Varieties

'Champion'
'Dutch'
'Lusitanica'
'Maliformis'
'Meech's Prolific'

Supports

Knock a short stake into the ground inside the planting hole and then plant the tree, spreading the roots around the post. Do not knock the post in after planting as this can damage the roots. Use a proprietary tree tie to support the trunk.

Initial training

Start with a young feathered tree. Clear the trunk of any laterals up to about 60cm (2ft) from ground level. Another 30cm (1ft) or so above this, cut back the leader just above a strong bud. Remove the tips of the remaining laterals, shortening them by up to two-thirds at an upward-facing bud. The following winter, cut back the new main leader just above a strong lateral about 30cm (1ft) above the previous winter's cut. This lateral will now become the top branch. Shorten the tips of all the other laterals by one-third to half of the previous year's growth.

Established pruning

Once the basic shape of the quince bush is established, it will continue to throw out new shoots. Unless they are filling in a gap, these should be removed, especially if they are crossing or crowding other branches and shoots. Keep the centre relatively open to allow in plenty of light and circulating air. As the tree ages, remove some of the older spurs to thin out congested clusters and new growth low down. Remove the tips of the leaders to promote spur production. If any laterals appear low down on the trunk, or suckers from its base, these should be removed.

LEFT Most quinces are grown on relatively small trees and this, along with their very decorative blossom and fruit, makes them an attractive tree for the small garden.

RIGHT A young quince in its second or third year. The laterals have been cut back to outward-facing buds so that it has bushed out nicely. One or two of the crossing and more vigorous shoots will have to be removed shortly.

TRAINING A QUINCE BUSH

Quinces are usually grown as bush trees, although they can be trained into other forms such as fans. They can grow as multi-stemmed trees but are best if they can be trained with a single trunk. They have a tendency to sucker and these should be removed. The suckers may appear from below ground or from the base of the trunk.

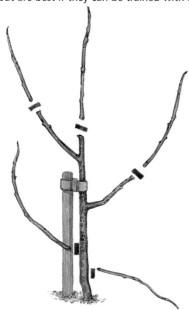

YEAR ONE, WINTER Plant a young feathered tree and cut off the leader at about 1m (3ft). Select two or four strong laterals at the top of the trunk and then remove all the other ones. Cut back the remainder by up to two-thirds.

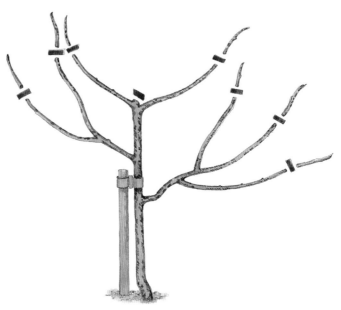

YEAR TWO, WINTER/SPRING Next winter or spring, cut out the new leader at about 30cm (1ft) above the previous cut and choose two more good laterals, making around five or so, removing any others. Cut back the branch leaders by one-third to half of the previous season's growth.

YEAR THREE, WINTER By the following winter the general shape should be becoming apparent. Remove any crossing, rubbing or misplaced shoots and keep the centre as open as possible.

ESTABLISHED PRUNING, WINTER In the established tree cut out any vigorous vertical growth along with any new shoots that are not required to fill an empty space. Remove the tips of the leaders.

FIGS (*Ficus carica*)
Fig bush

Figs form distinctive-looking trees. In warm areas, they can be grown as free-standing bushes, although it is quite common to see bushes trained against walls. These, however, are often fans that have grown wild through lack of pruning. A bush will grow up to about 4m (12ft) tall and the same across, and is worth having if you have the space and can provide the appropriate conditions.

Supports

Knock a sturdy post into the ground in the planting hole and spread the roots of the tree around it. Avoid knocking in the post after planting, as this can damage the roots. Use a proprietary tree tie to fasten it to the trunk. Restrict root growth by digging a hole 60cm (2ft) deep and across and lining the bottom and

sides with paving slabs, or use a large container, with plenty of small holes, sunk into the ground. Otherwise, the tree will reach a large size before producing much fruit.

Initial training

Plant a two-year-old tree in spring. Remove all the lower laterals below the ones you wish to keep as your lowest branch – probably around 60cm (2ft) from ground-level. Retain around six or seven branches and cut back the leader immediately above the top branch. This should be at about 1.2m (4ft). The next spring, remove any laterals that cross or crowd one another. In summer, pinch out the tips of all new shoots, restricting them to five or so leaves. This will expose the developing fruits to sunlight and so encourage them to open.

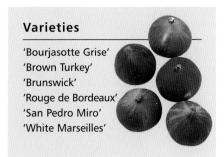

Varieties

'Bourjasotte Grise'
'Brown Turkey'
'Brunswick'
'Rouge de Bordeaux'
'San Pedro Miro'
'White Marseilles'

Established pruning

The main pruning should take place in early spring. Figs reshoot readily, so can be heavily pruned (even back to the ground) if necessary to restrict growth. The main aim is to keep the bush open. Remove any crossing or overcrowded stems, if possible cutting to upward-pointing shoots so that the tree grows upright rather than spreading. Cut out any dead or damaged wood. In summer, take out shoot tips as described.

TRAINING A FIG BUSH

In warmer districts, figs can be grown as bush trees in the open. When planting, it is important that you restrict their roots by

planting in a large container sunk into the ground, as this helps to restrain the tree's growth and encourage fruiting. It is best to

start the bush with a well-balanced feathered tree, as this will save at least a year over a maiden whip.

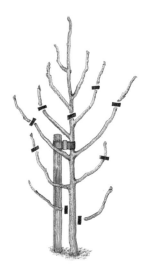

YEAR ONE, SPRING Plant the young feathered tree. Cut off the leader at about 1.2m (4ft), above the desired top branch. Cut off all laterals below the desired bottom branch, about 60cm (2ft) above the ground.

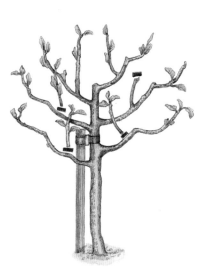

YEAR TWO, SPRING The following spring cut out all the crossing shoots and those not needed to form the framework of the tree. In the summer, cut back all new growth to five or six leaves.

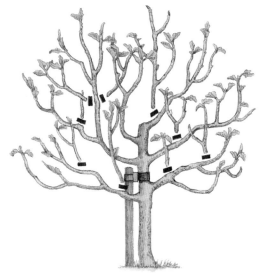

ESTABLISHED PRUNING, SPRING Once established, prune in spring, cutting out any crossing or unwanted shoots. If necessary, the bush can be cut back quite hard if it is becoming overgrown or taking up too much space. In summer, take out the shoot tips.

Fig fan

In cool areas figs grown as fans stand a better chance of producing a good crop of fruit, as the warmth of a wall will help to protect them. Figs are quite vigorous, even if the roots are restricted, so it is important to keep on top of the pruning and not let the fan degenerate into a tree.

Supports

Attach five to seven parallel wires, set about 30cm (12in) apart, preferably to a wall, though a solid fence will also do. Make certain that they are held at least 10cm (4in) away from the wall to allow air to circulate. The bottom wire should be about 45cm (18in) from ground-level. Restrict root growth by sinking 60cm (2ft) paving slabs into the ground around and underneath the root system. This helps to dwarf the tree and encourages it to bear fruit rather than putting on too much leafy growth. Alternatively, grow the fig in a large container.

Initial training

In the early spring, plant a two-year-old fig. The plant should have two strong laterals, the upper one around 38cm (15in) above ground-level, or just below the bottom wire. Train these shoots sideways, attached to canes tied in at an angle of about 40 degrees to the horizontal. Cut back the laterals to about 45cm (18in). Cut off the leader just above the higher of the two laterals. The following spring, cut back the new growth on the main branches and any new sub-laterals to about half their length. During the summer, tie in new growths to canes as they develop. The following winter, repeat the previous spring's steps, and reduce the lengths of all new growths. Remove any that grow towards or away from the wall, and take out any growth that will cause overcrowding. Aim for an even, relatively open spread. Stop all growths when they have filled the allotted space.

Established pruning

In spring, cut back shoots that have fruited to one bud. Prevent the tree from being overcrowded by removing crossing or crowding branches and shoots. Take out any dead or damaged wood. Remove the tips of any new branches that are extending beyond the allotted space.

TRAINING A FIG FAN

For most gardens in cooler areas the best way to grow figs is as a fan. They grow best against a wall, but can also be trained against a fence. Restrict the roots by planting in a container sunk into the ground. This will restrain the tree's growth. If the roots are allowed to grow freely, the plant will grow vigorously but will not produce much fruit.

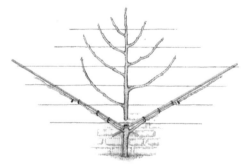

YEAR ONE, SPRING Plant a two-year-old feathered tree in early spring and cut the leader out just above two strong laterals. Tie the laterals to canes at 40 degrees and cut them back to about 45cm (18in).

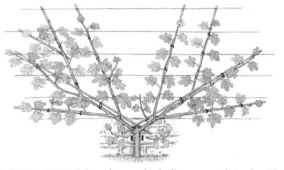

YEAR TWO, SPRING In spring, cut back all new growth to about half. In summer, tie the new growth to canes. In winter, repeat the previous spring's steps and reduce the length of all new growths. Remove unwanted growth.

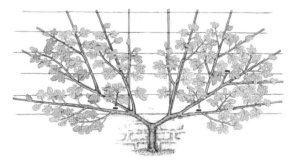

SUBSEQUENT YEARS Continue to follow this regime until the whole space is evenly filled with shoots. Keep the centre relatively clear and take out any vigorous vertical shoots.

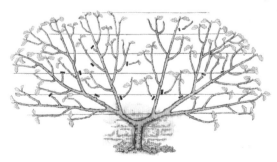

ESTABLISHED PRUNING, SPRING Once established, the main pruning in spring is to cut all fruited shoots back to one bud. As usual, also cut back any misplaced new shoots.

MEDLARS (*Mespilus germanica*)
Medlar tree

Medlars are grown mainly for their ornamental qualities and historical associations. They cannot be eaten directly from the tree but need, in effect, to be rotten before they become edible.

Support
Before planting, knock a short stake into the ground where the medlar is to be planted.

Initial training
Plant a young feathered tree and remove completely any laterals on the trunk up to a height of about 1.2m (4ft) above ground-level. Reduce the other laterals, below what

Varieties

'Bredase Reus'
'Dutch'
'Large Russian'
'Monstrous'
'Nottingham'
'Royal'

will be the lowest branch, by about half. The following winter, select the laterals that you want to form the basis of the crown of the tree, then remove the rest. If the tree has reached the height you wish the trunk to attain (probably about 2m/6ft), cut back the leader just

above the top lateral. If not, let it grow unpruned for another year. Remove any unwanted laterals. Also cut out any shoots that are crossing or crowding, especially any that are dominating the centre of the tree, which should be left open.

Established pruning
This is one of the easiest fruits to prune, as there is virtually nothing to do once the tree has matured. If necessary, remove any dead or damaged wood during late summer. Do not shorten, or tip-prune the horizontal branches, as this is likely to result in a lot of sucker growth, which will spoil the shape of the tree.

TRAINING A MEDLAR TREE
Because of their ornamental value, young medlar trees are still relatively easy to buy. Once established, they do not need much in the way of pruning and so are simple to look after. Start with a young feathered tree. Medlars make attractive specimen trees and can be planted in a decorative part of the garden rather than with other fruit or vegetables.

YEAR ONE, WINTER Plant the young tree in the winter and remove the lowest laterals. Reduce the other laterals, below what will eventually be the lowest branch, by about half.

YEAR TWO, WINTER In the second winter select the laterals that you wish to have as the branches. Cut the leader off above the top one and remove all other laterals below the bottom one.

ESTABLISHED PRUNING, WINTER By the third year the basic shape should have been formed, and established pruning only involves the removal of any misplaced wood and any shoots that appear on the trunk. If necessary, remove any dead or damaged wood in late summer.

MULBERRIES (*Morus* species)
Mulberry tree

Mulberries are in a category all on their own in that most will outlive the person who planted them – they can live for hundreds of years.

Supports
Hammer a strong stake into the ground to hold the tree straight in its early years. Put the stake in before planting so that you do not damage the roots.

Initial training
For an ornamental tree with a gnarled look, little needs to be done after planting, but for a more productive, better-shaped tree a little formative training helps. Prune only in the early part of winter, as any cuts will bleed if made at other times

Varieties
'Chelsea'
'King James'
'Large Black'
'Wellington'

of year. Plant either a maiden whip or a feathered tree. Remove the lower laterals up to about 1.2–1.5 (4–5ft) above ground-level once the tree has grown large enough and has several branches developing above the cleared trunk. A year later, cut the leader back above the lateral that you want to become the top branch. If you want it to grow into a tall tree, leave the main leader intact. The tree can now be left to develop naturally.

Established pruning
In general, there is no pruning to do on an established mulberry tree, other than cutting out any dead or damaged wood, which should be done in early to mid-winter. Any other branches that you have to take off for any reason should also be removed at this time of year. Very old mulberry trees often have a pronounced lean, and wooden props under at least one branch may be needed in order to prevent collapse. This lean can sometimes be apparent even at a relatively young age, and you may find that you have to put a stout prop under one of the branches yourself. However, far from being unsightly, this only adds to its venerable appearance.

TRAINING A MULBERRY TREE

Mulberries have become generally available once more and are not especially difficult to find. They are easy to look after because there is little pruning needed once they have been established, although in their old age they may well need some form of support, which usually takes the form of a prop because these trees have a tendency to lean.

YEAR ONE, WINTER Plant a feathered tree in winter and tie it to a firm stake. Remove any laterals below what you want as your lowest branch.

YEAR TWO, WINTER In the following winter cut out the leader just above what you want as the top branch. Leave it another year or two if you want a taller tree.

ESTABLISHED PRUNING No pruning of established trees is generally required, but very old trees may need to have stout props put under some of their sagging limbs to prevent them breaking or the tree collapsing entirely.

COBNUTS (*Corylus avellana*)
Cobnut tree

Cobnuts and filberts have a dual function: they are grown both for their decorative appearance and for their nutritious nuts. A third function can also be added: a well-developed cobnut makes a very pleasant tree to sit under. Decide what you want the tree to do. In nature, hazel tends to be a multi-stemmed tree and this form is the most decorative in the garden. Nuts will be produced on such a tree, but for greater numbers the trees are usually grown on a single, short stem, from which the main branches appear.

Supports

Generally no supports are required except for the initial planting if the site is exposed. Should that be the case, a short stake with a proprietary tree tie will suffice until the tree has become established.

Initial training

For a multi-stemmed bush, there is little else to do than to put in a young plant and let it develop, but for a tree a little more attention is required. It can be formed in the same way as many other bush fruit trees. Start with a one-year-old

ABOVE A cluster of developing cobnuts. They will need netting if there are any squirrels in the vicinity, or they will all disappear.

sapling. Cut back the tip to about 60cm (24in) above ground-level, just above a bud. The following year, a number of laterals will form. Select the top three or four of these and remove the rest to create a clear trunk of about 45cm (18in). Cut back each of the chosen laterals to about 25cm (10in) at a strong bud. In the third winter, remove the tips of all the main shoots to encourage further branching.

Established pruning

Keep the trunk below the main branches clear of growth. In late summer, snap all the new long, strong growths in half, being careful

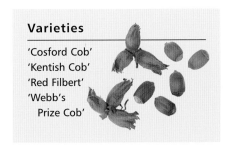

to break them only partially so that they hang down (a process known as "brutting"). This is not a particularly attractive method and is not recommended for ornamental varieties, but is an effective way of increasing the fruiting capacity of the tree. In early spring, as soon as you can see the small clusters of tiny red female flowers (much smaller than the yellow catkins that appear at the tips of the fruiting buds), cut back all the shoots, including the broken ones, to the first bunch of catkins or the first cluster of female flowers. If the shoot contains catkins only, leave until the catkins fade then remove it entirely. Also take out any dead, crossing or congested wood, keeping the centre of the tree open. As the tree matures, cut some of the older wood back to where there is suitable young growth.

PRUNING A COBNUT TREE

1 An old established cobnut tree, showing the ideal open goblet shape that you should aim for when pruning.

2 Some of the older growth can be removed to stimulate new growth and to open up the centre of the tree.

3 Remove growth that is going to cross and rub against other branches. Also remove any growth that is likely to cause congestion.

4 Inward-facing branches should be removed completely so that the open goblet shape of the tree is maintained.

TRAINING A COBNUT TREE

Cobnuts can be bought in their first year as maiden whips, without any side shoots. Care is needed to ensure that they are properly trained otherwise they may develop into multi-stemmed shrubs rather than trees. This will not be a disaster, but for nut production, trees are better. Multi-stemmed shrubs are in turn much easier and more decorative to grow.

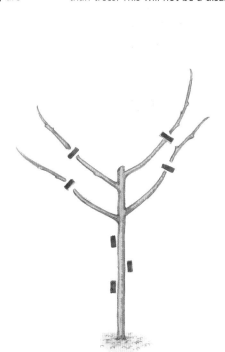

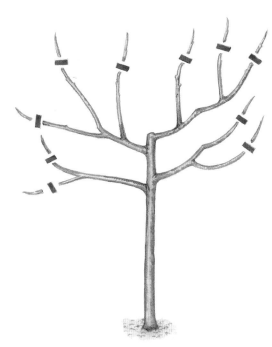

YEAR ONE, WINTER Plant a sapling in the winter and cut off the leader at the height where you want the top of the trunk to be, at about 60cm (24in).

YEAR TWO, WINTER In the second winter decide which laterals you want to create the branches, and remove the rest. Cut back the chosen laterals to about 25cm (10in) or so.

SUBSEQUENT WINTERS In the following winters until the tree is fully developed, cut out the tips of the shoots to provoke further branching.

BRUTTING, SUMMER It is normal to "brut" established trees in late summer. Snap all the long growth in half, but do not break them completely. Leave them hanging, although they might look untidy.

BRUTTING, SPRING In early spring, prune these broken stems back to just above the first tiny red flower you can see. If the shoot has only catkins, wait till they fade and then remove the shoot completely.

WALNUTS *(Juglans* species)
Walnut tree

Walnuts were often grown as hedgerow plants, the only attention given being the gathering of the walnuts once they were shed. Today, they are grown by discriminating gardeners who have enough room for them. Walnut trees tend to grow large but are extremely decorative.

Varieties

'Broadview'
'Buccaneer'
'Franquette'
'Mayette'

Supports
Support is needed only for the first couple of years until the tree is well established, after which it can be dispensed with. A stake knocked into the ground and a proprietary tree tie are all that is required.

Initial training
Walnuts can be purchased as feathered trees in containers for planting in late autumn to early winter. The best time for all pruning is autumn to early winter, after the wood has matured. Pruning at other times results in copious sap bleeding from the wounds. In the autumn after planting, remove some of the lower laterals. A year later, if the tree has grown enough, remove all the laterals from the trunk below those that will form the lowest branches. For a tree with a leader, the most commonly grown form, allow this to continue to grow unpruned. For a more rounded tree, remove the leader above the required topmost branch. Often the leader is stopped by frost or wind damage. In this case, two leaders will probably now develop. Left as they are, the tree will not grow quite so tall, but if you want to continue with a central leader, rub out one of the two buds beneath the damaged tip (if they have already started growing, cut out one of the new replacement shoots). Other than removing any crossing or congested wood, allow the tree to develop in its own time.

Established pruning
Very little is required other than to remove any dead, diseased or damaged wood and to cut back any crossing wood.

TRAINING A WALNUT TREE

Walnuts are usually grown as standard trees, either tall with a leader, or as a more rounded shape with branches radiating from the top of the trunk. They bleed easily, so pruning should take place in autumn to early winter.

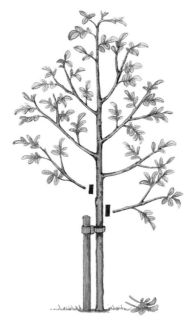

YEAR ONE, AUTUMN/WINTER Plant a feathered tree in late autumn to early winter and the following autumn remove the lower laterals to form a clear trunk up to 60cm (2ft).

YEAR TWO, AUTUMN A year later, in autumn, repeat the exercise and remove a few more laterals, up to 1.2m (4ft). The lowest remaining ones will now form the lowest branches.

ESTABLISHED PRUNING Once established, very little pruning is required except to remove any dead or damaged wood. Any crossing wood can also be removed.

SWEET CHESTNUTS *(Castanea sativa)*
Sweet chestnut tree

The other nut tree that is commonly grown in cooler climates is the sweet chestnut. However, it is grown mainly for its timber, the nuts being incidental. The best nuts are to be found on trees that are grown in hotter regions. However, a number of cultivars that reliably produce fruit are now available.

Supports
Generally none is required, but a single stake may be advisable for the first couple of years in more exposed positions, while the tree is establishing.

Initial training
When buying, ensure that you ask for sweet chestnut *(Castanea sativa)* and specify that you want it for the

Varieties

'Laguépie'
'Marron de Lyon'
'Marron de Redon'
'Marigoule'

nuts so that you get a good cultivar – some particularly decorative forms produce inferior nuts. Generally, sweet chestnut trees are allowed to develop into a central-leader standard. Allow a feathered tree with a strong leader to develop, removing the lower laterals at the height you wish the lower branches to be. Other than removing any crossing or unwanted laterals as the tree establishes, it can be left to develop on its own.

Sweet Chestnut timber

Chestnut produces very good timber for stakes and poles for garden use, or larger poles for constructing arbours or fences. If the tree is trained as a multi-stemmed stool, it will produce a number of poles every few years. Cut these to within 30cm (12in) or so of ground-level. More shoots will then develop.

Established pruning
Little pruning is required once the tree is established other than to remove any dead or damaged wood. The trees will start to produce fruit in quantity after about ten years. In maturity, a sweet chestnut can shed limbs, and any such breakages should be neatly trimmed.

TRAINING A SWEET CHESTNUT

Sweet chestnut trees are usually planted for timber in cooler countries but increasingly stock suitable for fruiting trees is being offered. This is usually in the form of feathered trees. Once established, the tree needs little in the way of pruning.

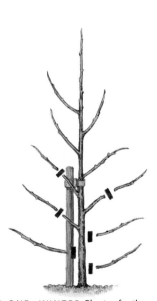

YEAR ONE, WINTER Plant a feathered tree in winter. Remove the lowest branches, up to about 60cm (2ft), and cut back the higher ones, up to 1.2m (4ft), by about half of their length.

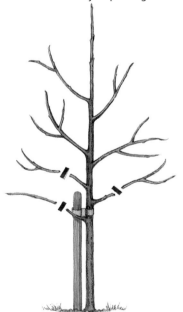

YEAR TWO, WINTER In the following winter cut out completely those laterals that were cut in half last winter. If the trunk is still not tall enough, cut more laterals in half, up to the desired lowest branches.

SUBSEQUENT YEARS Once the height of the cleared trunk has been reached, remove any remaining stubs. The tree will grow for many years and need very little pruning, other than to keep the shape balanced.

Soft Fruit

Soft fruit has always been one of the mainstays of the garden, even the small one. One reason for this is that while tree fruit can be stored and easily transported, soft fruit tastes much better eaten straight from the bush, or at least within a short time of picking. Commercially produced fruit can never compare with your own. Even a few canes of raspberries, for example, will provide a surprising amount of fruit, and there is often enough to freeze some for the future, or to make into jam.

Soft fruit is relatively easy to look after as long as pruning takes place regularly. If neglected, the bushes or canes can become an unproductive, tangled mess. Pruning them is not arduous or complicated once you have grasped the basic principles. There are two important aspects that must be given equal attention if you are to succeed. The first is to control weeds, which are not a problem that usually affects tree fruit. They must be kept at bay and prevented from climbing up through the plants. The other problem is birds, who are as fond of raspberries and blackberries as we are. Some form of protection is necessary if you are to get a good crop.

LEFT Luscious blackberries that make your mouth water simply by looking at them. As with most fruit, they always taste that much better when freshly picked.

Growing soft fruit

Soft fruit is not difficult to grow, nor is the initial training and subsequent pruning tricky. The canes and bushes can be easily purchased and will usually produce at least some fruit in the first year. Siting and conditions are important, most requiring a reasonably rich, moisture-retentive but not waterlogged soil. Although all need sun, few require great heat and they can easily be grown in cooler areas.

ABOVE Tayberries are one of the several hybrid berries that are worth experimenting with for new tastes. They are not difficult to grow.

ABOVE Blackberry canes can use spaces that might otherwise be wasted. Here they are supported on a fence by an old shed.

Buying

All soft fruit is readily available from garden centres or specialist nurseries. The latter give a much larger range of choice and often better advice. If, for example, you wanted to grow raspberries from early summer through to late autumn, then a specialist nursery will be able to advise on which varieties are most suitable to give you a constant flow of fruit. Although it is possible to propagate your own from existing stock, it is generally better to start with fresh, certified stock every few years to prevent the build-up of disease.

Planting

The canes or young bushes are usually supplied in late autumn for winter or early spring planting. (Frequently, those from specialist nurseries are bare-rooted. If they cannot be planted straight away, heel them into the soil until they are required.) The soil should be well dug, with plenty of well-rotted organic material incorporated into it.

For fruit bushes that need support, raspberries and blackberries for example, it is best to erect the wirework first to avoid damaging the newly planted canes. Look for the soil mark on the stems and plant to the same depth as they were grown in the nursery beds.

Supports

Cane fruit will need support, usually provided in the form of wires tightly stretched between posts. Over time these can slacken as the wire stretches, so it is advisable to make the wires adjustable, using bottle-screw tighteners, for example. The posts are likely to be in place for a number of years, so if they are wood,

ABOVE A selection of delicious fruit from the garden. From top left: red currants, strawberries, blackcurrants, raspberries, blackberries and gooseberries.

ABOVE Most soft fruit needs to be pruned back once it has been planted. The stems on sold plants are generally too long.

ABOVE A large garden is not necessary for fruit-growing. This method of growing red currants produces a good crop that is bird-proofed.

treat them first to prevent them rotting. Bush fruit generally does not need supporting unless you are training it into a decorative form such as a fan or a standard. In the case of the former, wires supported by a wall or sturdy fence are best. A standard needs a stake or strong cane to support it, at least during the formative years and often throughout its life.

ABOVE When cutting out the dead canes from raspberries and blackberries, cut as low as possible and try not to leave too many snags.

GROWING SOFT FRUIT ON POSTS AND WIRES

1 Use strong posts to form the framework for supporting soft fruit. Knock the posts firmly into the ground using a mallet so that they do not wobble.

2 A brace set at an angle of 45 degrees will help to keep the post stable as well as prevent it from tipping under the strain of the wires.

3 The wire can be initially drawn tight by hand and partially stapled into position. It should then be tightened with a strainer and the staples hammered home.

4 Soft string can be used to tie in the canes. This should preferably pass between the wire and the stem in order to prevent any chafing which will damage the plant.

Initial training

Cane fruit is usually trained from the start as it will go on being trained. Most bush fruits are generally grown as open bushes, which need to be of good shape and relatively open with no cross-overs or congested growth. Many can also be trained in more decorative ways, such as cordons, espaliers, fans and even, in some cases, standards. These require a bit more attention to keep them in shape. Individual requirements will be given for each type of fruit.

Established pruning

Dead canes should be removed every year and new ones tied in to the supports. Bush fruit also needs a little attention each year to ensure that the bushes stay healthy and productive. The techniques vary for each type of fruit as is detailed on the following pages.

The pruning cuts are the same as already discussed for all other plants. They should be made just above a bud so there is no snag, and should preferably slope away from the bud at about 30 degrees.

CANE FRUITS
Raspberries *(Rubus idaeus)*

Raspberries are not difficult to grow and with the right selection of varieties the fruit is produced over a long season, often continuing until the first winter frosts. It is possible to grow just a few canes tied together at the top, with a net thrown over them to keep the birds off, but they are more often grown in rows, preferably in a fruit cage.

Varieties

Raspberries	Mid-season	'Augusta'
Early	'Glen Lyon'	'Leo'
'Delight'	'Glen Prosen'	'Malling'
'Glen Coe'	'Julia'	'Malling Joy'
'Glen Cova'	'Malling Jewel'	
'Glen Moy'	'Malling Orion'	*Autumn*
'Malling Exploit'		'Autumn Bliss'
'Malling Promise'	*Late*	'Fallgold'	'Norfolk Giant'
'Sumner'	'Admiral'	'Heritage'	'September'

Supports

Raspberries are usually planted in rows. Each cane is supported against horizontal wires, which are held in place by sturdy posts at 2.5–3m (8–10ft) intervals. The bottom wire is at about 60cm (2ft), with two more wires above that at the same intervals of 60cm (2ft). The wires should be stretched as tight as possible and should have bottle screws or some other method of tightening them in case they start to slacken. Rows should be 2m (6ft) apart. Plant the young canes at 60cm (2ft) intervals, in well-prepared soil, between late autumn and early spring. Usually, the canes will have been cut back to about 60cm (2ft) when you buy them. If not, trim them back and tie into the bottom wire so that they do not blow over while the roots are establishing.

Summer-fruiting raspberries

In spring, new canes are produced. Tie these into the wires in an upright position. Once the new canes have started growing, the old canes from the previous year can be cut back to the base. If the canes are extra long, bend them over and tie their tips down. At the end of winter, cut off the arching tips, leaving about 15cm (6in) above the top wire. During the summer, these canes will fruit, and at the same time a new set of canes will arise from the base. Once they canes have finished fruiting, cut these off at the base and tie the new ones in their place in a continuous cycle. Remove any new suckering growth between the rows.

Autumn-fruiting raspberries

The autumn varieties are dealt with differently. If they are treated in the same manner as summer-fruiting types they will fruit in the same way. However, they are normally pruned in the spring to produce an autumn crop. The newly planted canes will produce growth during their first summer that will produce fruit in the autumn. As they grow, tie them in to the wires, although some of the shorter forms are almost self-supporting. Towards the end of winter, cut all canes to the ground. New ones will appear and these should be tied in. Fruit will appear on these in autumn and they can be cut back again the following late winter, in a continuous cycle. Some new varieties of autumn-fruiting raspberry fruit both in the autumn and again in the following summer on the same canes. Leave these canes unpruned until after their second crop, which means in effect that they are trained and pruned like summer-fruiting raspberries. Check when you buy which type you have.

PRUNING AUTUMN RASPBERRIES

1 Autumn raspberries are pruned differently from summer raspberries. As with ordinary raspberries, during the winter they consist of a mixture of fruited and new canes.

2 Regardless of what they are, the canes are all cut to the ground and completely removed.

3 Once the canes have been cut back, new growth quickly appears. Once the canes are tall enough, they should be tied in to supporting wires.

TRAINING RASPBERRIES

Some of the shorter autumn varieties can be grown without wire supports, but all other raspberries are best given a post-and-wire support, and grown in open ground rather than against a fence or wall. Raspberries are best planted in winter from plants that have been newly purchased because unlike existing canes, these will be disease-free.

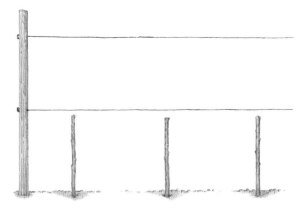

YEAR ONE, WINTER Often the canes will have been cut back by the nursery. If not, cut back to 60cm (2ft) and tie them to the bottom wire.

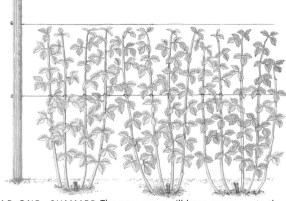

YEAR ONE, SUMMER The new canes will have grown up to the top wires, and should be tied to the supports.

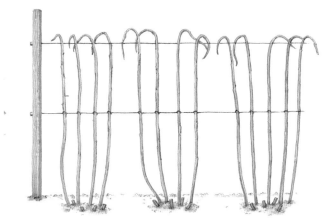

SUMMER-FRUITING RASPBERRIES, YEAR TWO, WINTER In the early winter cut out the remains of the old stems. Pull the tips of the new canes over and tie them to the wires.

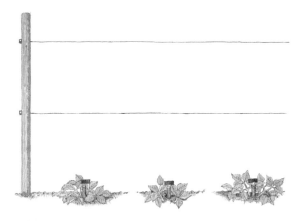

AUTUMN-FRUITING RASPBERRIES, YEAR TWO, WINTER Cut all canes to the ground. The result may look drastic, but the tufts of new growth will soon appear and produce a crop through to late autumn.

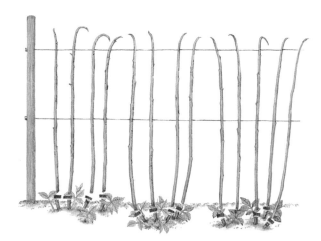

AUTUMN-FRUITING RASPBERRIES, YEAR TWO, SUMMER New canes will have grown up to the top wires and should be tied to the supports.

ABOVE A ripening crop of 'Glen Rosa' raspberries. When picking raspberries, gently squeeze them between finger and thumb and ease away from their stalk, the remains of two of which can be seen here.

Blackberries (*Rubus fruticosus*) and hybrid berries

Blackberries and hybrid berries are usually grown in the same way. They both occupy considerable space. Although derived from wild blackberries, cultivated varieties usually produce larger and sweeter fruit. The hybrid berries, such as loganberries and tayberries, have usually been crossed with another similar fruit. Some varieties are thornless, which is a great advantage when harvesting.

Varieties

Blackberries
'Ashton Cross'
'Bedford Giant' – early
'Himalayan Giant'
'John Innes'
'Loch Ness'
'Merton Early'
'Merton Thornless'
'Oregon Thornless'
'Smoothstem'
'Thornfree'

blackberries

Hybrid berries
Boysenberry
Hildaberry
Japanese wineberry
Loganberry
Marionberry
Sunberry
Tayberry
Worcesterberry

tayberries

Supports

A sturdy post-and-wire system is required, with the posts being set at about 3m (10ft) intervals. Four or five wires, about 30cm (12in) apart, should be stretched between them, the lowest being about 45cm (18in) from the ground. They can also be grown against fences, making a useful impenetrable barrier.

Initial and subsequent training

There are several ways to train blackberries and hybrid berries, all essentially similar but differing in detail. Basically, the previous year's growth (on which the fruit will be carried) is tied in to the wires, while the current year's growth is kept separate. After fruiting, all fruited wood is cut out and the current year's wood tied in to

replace it. One of the easiest methods is the one-way or alternate bay system. The canes are trained along the wires either to the right or left of the plant, but only in one direction. Depending on the number of canes, each wire will support one or more. As it grows, the current year's growth is tied in to the wires on the opposite side of the plant. After fruiting, all the

TRAINING METHODS FOR BLACKBERRIES AND HYBRID BERRIES

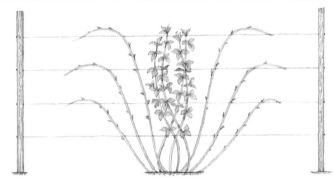

FAN TRAINING The new canes are temporarily tied vertically and along the top wire, while the fruiting canes are tied in singly along the wires. Any excess canes are removed. After fruiting, these canes are taken out and the new growth tied in their place.

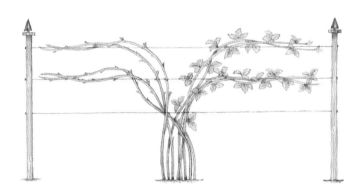

ALTERNATE BAY One way in which you can train blackberries is to tie all the new growth to one side of the wirework. After fruiting, remove the previous year's growth from the other side and then use this for the next year's new growth. Repeat each year.

Thornless blackberry blossom

Blackberries

Hildaberry flowers

canes on the fruited side are cut out and during the second year the new growth is tied in to replace them. This is a good method for prickly varieties, as the canes only have to be handled once.

For cultivars that produce long, vigorous stems, the canes can be woven along the wires on either side in a snakelike manner, either running parallel to each other or alternating. The new growth is tied in two bundles along the top wire. After fruiting, the old canes are cut off at the base and the bundles are untied for weaving in a similar manner to the previous year's canes.

With less vigorous varieties, the fruiting canes can be tied in a straight line against the wires (no weaving), with the following year's canes tied in a column at the centre.

ABOVE New shoots should be tied in as they grow, otherwise they will thrash around and cause damage to themselves and other plants.

After fruiting, the old canes are removed and the new ones tied in their place.

Established pruning

As the years pass, the plants may produce more canes than there is space for, so you may need to thin the current year's growth. Take out

ABOVE Tayberries tied in using the alternative bay method, with all the new shoots tied to the right and last year's removed from the left.

any thin or weak canes. Try to ensure that the canes are tied in properly for the winter or they may thrash around in the wind and be damaged. They should be tied in all year round, as any tips that touch the ground may well root, creating another clump. Blackberries form thickets if not kept under control.

WEAVING This is a good method of training blackberries where space is short. The current year's fruiting growth is woven up and over two or three wires, while the following year's fruiting canes are all temporarily tied in to the top wire.

ROPE TRAINING A second way to train blackberries is to temporarily tie in all new growth vertically to the wirework and along the top wire. The current fruiting canes are tied in groups horizontally. These are removed after fruiting and the new growth tied in their place.

Japanese wineberry

Hildaberries

Tayberries

BUSH FRUITS
Blackcurrants *(Ribes nigrum)*

Blackcurrants are a popular garden fruit because of their high vitamin content. One bush is often sufficient to provide enough fresh fruit and some left over for the freezer. Although red and white currants appear similar, apart from the colour of the fruit, they have a different pruning regime, so do not apply the same techniques to them all.

Supports

Blackcurrants do not need supports. However, the bushes need netting to prevent birds stealing the fruit. One or two bushes can be netted individually but it is more practical to grow blackcurrants in a fruit cage.

Initial training

Plants are often sold bare-rooted. If you cannot plant them in their final position straight away, heel them in temporarily in some spare ground. Plant to the same depth, or fractionally lower, as they were grown

ABOVE A trug of freshly picked blackcurrants. Even one bush will produce a surprising quantity of currants.

Varieties

Blackcurrants	'Ben Sarek'
'Baldwin'	'Boskoop Giant'
'Ben Connan'	'Malling Jet'
'Ben Lomond'	'Mendip Cross'
'Ben More'	'Wellington XXX'

in the nursery (look for the soil mark on the stems), then cut them back to a bud roughly 5cm (2in) above ground-level. This will result in the production of strong new shoots in the following year. These can be left unpruned, but you will need to cut out any weak ones. Fruit will appear on these shoots in their second year, and new growth will begin to develop from the base of the plant. In winter, cut out about one-third of the old fruited wood and any weak shoots.

PRUNING A YOUNG BLACKCURRANT ON PLANTNG

1 A newly planted blackcurrant bush before it is pruned.

2 First remove any weak growth, cutting it right out and removing old wood if necessary.

3 Finish by cutting back the longer shoots by half to a strong outward-facing shoot.

ABOVE It is important that you always cut out any dead or diseased wood, using a saw for thicker material.

ABOVE Cut out up to four of the oldest stems each year and cut the remainder of the fruited branches back to a new shoot.

ABOVE The remaining previous year's growth must be thinned out slightly to provide an open bush so that air and light can enter.

Established pruning

The fruit of blackcurrant bushes is carried on the previous year's or older wood. Older wood, however, progressively loses its ability to fruit well, so some of the oldest fruited wood should be removed every year to ensure that new wood will be produced and the bush revitalized.

Each year, between fruiting and the following spring, cut out two or three of the old branches completely. You also need to cut back some of the remaining older wood to vigorous new side shoots. Remove any branches or side-branches that are close to the ground and thin out the centre of the bush so that light enters and air can freely circulate.

PRUNING BLACKCURRANTS

With blackcurrants the fruit is carried on the previous year's or older wood. For this reason, it is important not to over-prune or

all the fruiting wood will be removed. However, it will be necessary to prune out older wood.

YEAR ONE, WINTER After planting, completely cut out any weak wood and reduce the other shoots to about 5cm (2in) or so above ground-level.

YEAR ONE, SUMMER The following summer, growth will spring from these reduced shoots, as well as completely new growth from the base. Cut out any weak shoots.

YEAR TWO, WINTER In the winter, cut out one-third of the old wood and any weak or damaged shoots to the base.

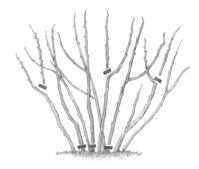

ESTABLISHED PRUNING, WINTER Once established, cut out up to four of the oldest branches each winter and then cut back the remaining fruited branches to a strong shoot.

Jostaberries

The jostaberry is an interesting hybrid between blackcurrants and gooseberries. It is treated in exactly the same way as blackcurrants in terms of training and pruning.

Red and white currants (*Ribes sativum*)

Red and white currants are variations of the same fruit. They are pruned in the same way, but differently to blackcurrants. As well as bushes, you can train red currants into decorative forms, such as cordons, espaliers, fans and standards.

Supports

Bush forms do not need any support but the more decorative forms need training, using wires against a wall or fence, or stretched between posts. Standards need a stake or a stout cane.

Initial training

Choose a strong-growing one-year-old plant with four good main branches on the main stem, about 10–12cm (4–5in) above the soil. Remove any other branches and

Varieties

Red currants	White currants
'Jonkheer van Tets'	'Versailles Blanche'
'Junifer'	'White Dutch'
'Laxton's Number 1'	'White Grape'
'Red Lake'	'White Pearl'
'Redstart'	
'Rondom'	
'Rovada'	

red currants   white currants

reduce these four by about half their length, cutting to an outward-facing bud. In the second winter, prune back all the new leaders by about half. Choose the best outward shoots on each of the main branches and cut these back by a half. Reduce any remaining shoots to a couple of buds. Any badly placed shoots that cross or are congested should be removed.

Established pruning

Remove the tips of all the main leaders and, once the framework of the plant has developed, you will need to cut back all subsequent side shoots to one bud. Every few years, remove a couple of main branches that have become unproductive, cutting back to a strong shoot.

Decorative forms

Red and white currants can be grown in a number of decorative forms. Cordons, espaliers and fans are trained and pruned in a very similar way to the method used for spur-producing apples. The aim is to create single or multiple cordons with one, two or three uprights bearing spurs rather than branches. Fans are slightly more complicated but basically similar. Develop two strong laterals from near the base and spread these out at an angle of about 40 degrees. Allow more shoots to develop from these until an even covering of the wall or fence is achieved. Reduce all other side shoots to one bud to produce fruiting spurs, and prune to maintain this. A standard can be achieved by grafting a red currant bush on to the stem of a vigorous currant stock. Treat the resulting top growth in the same way as you would for a normal bush, but keep it more compact. Remove any side shoots that appear on the main stem.

MULTIPLE CORDON This has two or more vertical stems. Start by cutting back a shrub to three shoots and train two horizontally and one vertically. Then treat as individual cordons.

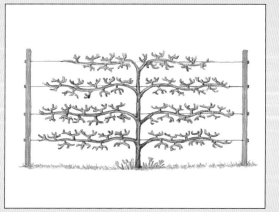

ESPALIER This is produced in the same way as an apple or pear espalier. Once the espalier is formed the individual arms are treated in the same way as the cordons.

STANDARD This is best bought ready formed, or it can be created by grafting a red currant on to a flowering currant rootstock and treating it as a bush currant.

TRAINING A RED CURRANT BUSH

Red currants are different to blackcurrants because they are spur-fruiting and so a permanent framework has to be built up.

This can be done in bush or cordon form or in a more decorative way (see the panel on the opposite page). Red currants are best

grown in a fruit cage in order to prevent marauding birds removing the delicious crop of currants.

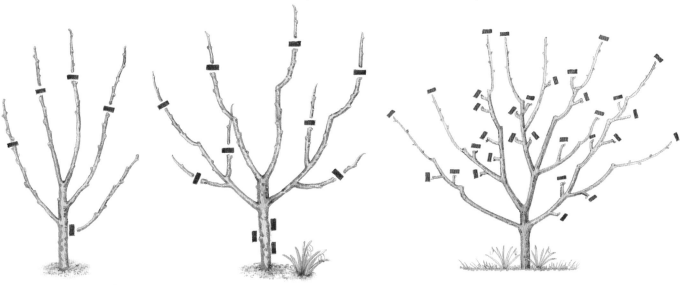

YEAR ONE, WINTER Plant a new bush. Select four well-placed branches and remove the rest. Reduce the remaining branches to half their length.

YEAR TWO, WINTER In the second winter, prune back the new growth on all the leaders by about half, cutting back to an outward-facing bud.

ESTABLISHED PRUNING, WINTER Once established, each winter cut back the tips of all the leaders and cut back any side shoots to one or two buds.

TRAINING A RED CURRANT CORDON

Red and white currants grown as cordons can save a great deal of space and so are particularly good for a small

garden. They are easier to net as individual plants and so do not necessarily need a fruit cage.

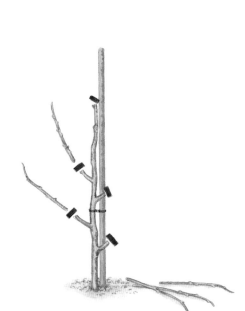
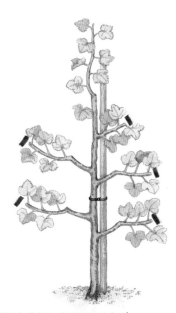
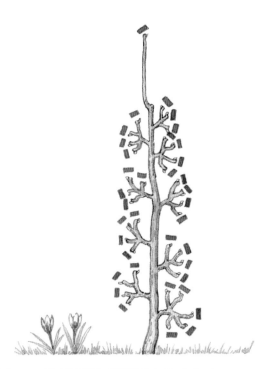

YEAR ONE, WINTER Start with a two-year-old plant and cut back all the side shoots to two buds. Then cut the new growth of the leader back by a half.

YEAR ONE, SUMMER In the summer take out the tips of the side shoots, cutting back to about five or six leaves.

YEAR TWO, WINTER In the following winter, cut back all the side shoots to one or two buds. Repeat the process every year.

Gooseberries *(Ribes uva-crispum)*

Although quite different in bush and fruit, gooseberries are often bracketed with red currants, as they are treated in the same way. There are a number of dessert varieties, but most gardeners grow them for culinary use. They have vicious thorns that can catch on skin, hair and clothes, so it is essential to wear tough gloves when pruning.

Supports

Gooseberries are normally grown as free-standing bushes, but they can also be grown as cordons, fans or standards. The first two methods need wires attached to walls or fences or stretched between stout posts.

Varieties

'Bedford Red'	'Lancashire Lad'
'Broom Girl'	'Leveller'
'Careless'	'Whinham's
'Early Sulphur'	Industry'
'Greenfinch'	'White Lion'
'Invicta'	'Whitesmith'
'Jubilee'	'Yellow Champagne'

Initial training

As with red currants, the first task when training gooseberries is to create a basic framework consisting of three or four main branches with several side branches, creating a well-clothed but not too dense shrub. Choose a good plant with a short (10–12cm/4–5in) leg from the top of which emerge three or four strong shoots. Cut these back to about half their length to upward-facing buds. The following winter, cut back all the new leaders and any strong side shoots that you want to keep for the framework by about

Decorative forms

Gooseberries can be grown as cordons and fans, which are not only decorative but also kinder on the hands when it comes to picking the fruit, as you do not have to thrust your hand into the bush. The different forms are developed in the same way as for apples, with single or multiple stems for cordons and an array of branches, all starting from two initial stems that are spread out at an angle of 40 degrees or so, for fans. Once the cordon stems or the branch structure of the fan have been developed, prune all shoots back to one bud to create a spur system.

Standard gooseberries are produced by grafting a bush on to a tall, vigorous currant stem. Once the bush has developed, it is pruned in the same way as for a free-standing bush, although it is best to keep it more compact to prevent wind rock.

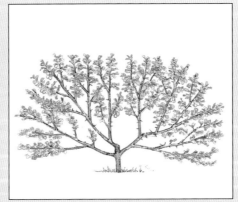

SINGLE CORDON Cordons can be created in much the same way as red and white currant cordons, building up a spur stytem.

MULTIPLE CORDON This can be created in exactly the same way as a single cordon, except that at the outset you will need to allow three shoots to develop, two of which should be trained horizontally and one vertically.

FAN This is a very decorative method of growing gooseberries. A gooseberry fan can be trained in the same way, although on a smaller scale, to a pear fan. Again, the basic idea is to form a good structure of spurs.

STANDARD It is best to buy standards already formed, but you can graft a gooseberry on to a flowering currant stem and then treat the top growth as an ordinary gooseberry bush, keeping the main stem bare.

ABOVE Start picking gooseberries before the first berries are fully ripe in order to give the remainder an opportunity to ripen.

one-third, also to upward-facing buds. Cut back the rest to one bud. Remember that you will have to put your hand right into the plant to harvest the fruit, so keep the bush relatively open with the minimum amount of congestion.

Established training

Once established, the simplest way of pruning is to cut back all new growth every winter to one bud, so that a system of spurs is built up similar to that of apples. Cut out any congested or crossing growth and occasionally take out an old branch back to a strong shoot. Some gardeners prefer to remove all the older wood to promote new growth, allowing the fruit to appear on this once it is two years old. It is important that you always try to keep the centre of the bush open. This will not only allow in light and air, but will also make it easier to pick and prune.

RIGHT Gooseberries make excellent cordons. Train them up canes that are supported by horizontal wires.

TRAINING GOOSEBERRIES

The main point to remember about gooseberries is the vicious thorns; you will need to wear a pair of stout leather gloves when tackling them. It is easiest to start with a two-year-old bush. Keep the bush open in order to make it easier to pick the fruit without pricking your hands. Growing gooseberry bushes is similar to the method for growing red currants.

YEAR ONE, WINTER Plant the gooseberry bush in the winter. Select three or four well-placed branches and remove the rest. Cut back the remainder of the branches by about half their length.

YEAR TWO, WINTER In the following winter, cut back all the new growth on the leaders and any new shoots you want to keep by one-third. Cut back the rest to one bud.

ESTABLISHED PRUNING Once established, keep the shrub as open as possible. Cut back all new growth to one bud in order to build up the spurs and, once it begins to age, remove some of the older growth to rejuvenate the bush.

Blueberries (*Vaccinium corymbosum*)

Blueberries are becoming ever more popular, and several varieties are now available. They form multi-stemmed bushes which, once established, will provide masses of fruit. The type that is most commonly grown is known as the highbush blueberry. Blueberries must have acid soil, but can be grown in containers filled with ericaceous compost if your garden soil is alkaline.

Varieties

'Berkeley'
'Bluecrop'
'Bluejay'
'Bluetta'
'Duke'
'Goldtraube'
'Herbert'
'Patriot'
'Spartan'

ABOVE In general, blueberries are left to grow in their natural state with little pruning when they will provide clusters of delicious berries.

Supports

No supports are necessary but some means of netting plants is essential if you hope to get to the fruit before the birds do. The ideal is to grow them in a fruit cage, but it is possible to drape a net over individual bushes while they are in fruit.

TRAINING BLUEBERRIES

Blueberries are very easy to look after and need little pruning, even during their formative stage. They are usually bought as

Initial training

Blueberry bushes are sold as one- or two-year-old plants that have been grown from cuttings. There is little to do after planting and for the first few years. Let them develop naturally, restricting pruning and taking out any weak growth or stems that cross or create congestion. Also

one- or two-year-olds and planted in the winter or early spring. Blueberries need an acid soil. If they are grown in chalky or

remove any shoots that develop horizontally. Aim to produce an upright plant.

Established pruning

Remove a few of the oldest stems to rejuvenate the plant. Also cut out any spreading branches, or those that cross and create congestion.

limestone areas, then they should be grown in containers rather than in the open ground.

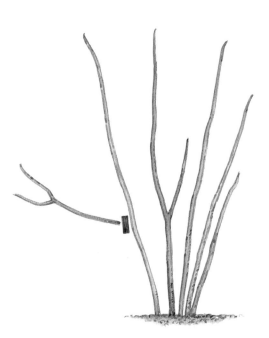

YEAR ONE, WINTER Plant the new blueberry bush in the winter and remove any weak, damaged or obviously wayward shoots. Otherwise allow to develop naturally.

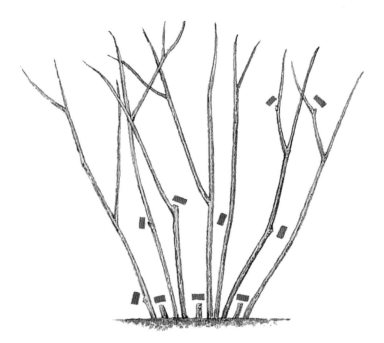

ESTABLISHED PRUNING, WINTER Once established take out one or two of the oldest stems to rejuvenate the plant and perhaps cut back any crossing or misplaced stems. Do not let the bush become too dense.

Cranberries (*Vitis macrocarpon*)

Cranberries are less widely grown than blueberries, but have become popular on account of their vitamin content as well as their culinary use. Several different varieties are available. Like blueberries, they thrive only on acid soils, but suitable conditions can be created in raised beds or in containers.

Support
Cranberries are low plants that are adapted to windy situations, so no support is required.

Initial training
After planting, allow the bushes to develop naturally. Cut out any dead or damaged wood as it appears.

Established pruning
Little attention is needed beyond keeping the site weed-free. Cranberry bushes send out runners and can create large colonies, but an excess of these reduces productivity. Prune out excess runners in spring, leaving just enough to extend the colony and fill gaps. Also remove some of the old uprights. If you have a large planting of cranberries, shears can be used for this, as long as you do not remove too much of the plant.

Varieties

'Early Black'
'Franklin'
'Hamilton'
'MacFarlin'
'Pilgrim'

The bilberry or whortleberry (*Vaccinium myrtillus*) and the European cranberry (*V. oxycoccos*) can be grown in the same way.

ABOVE Cranberries are popular because of their health-enhancing properties. They can be eaten as fruit or in juice and used in cooking.

ESTABLISHED PRUNING Little pruning is required other than shearing over the plant to remove some of the old uprights. The runners can also be removed to prevent congestion.

ABOVE Cranberries are healthy to eat and make an attractive plant in the kitchen garden.

ABOVE Commercial wet harvesting of cranberries. The plants are submerged in water and then the plants beaten so that the berries float off. They are then rounded up.

CLIMBING FRUIT
Grapes (*Vitis vinifera*)

Grapes are generally grown outside, but, in cooler climates, dessert types are usually best under glass. Wine grapes can easily be grown outside in cooler regions, provided the ripening fruits have adequate exposure to sunlight.

Rootstocks

After the incidence of phylloxera, a disease that ravaged French vineyards in the late nineteenth century, grape vines have nearly always, with a few minor exceptions, been grafted on to a resistant rootstock. This means that it is almost certain that you will be offered grafted plants. There are a number of different rootstocks, but it is likely that you will be supplied with those that are most suited to your region. If in doubt, check with your supplier, who can usually also recommend the most suitable variety of grape for your area.

Growing methods

Grapes need well-drained soil and a position exposed to the sun. They are trained on systems of posts and wires. Since grapevines have a long

Varieties

Outdoor varieties
'Brant' black, wine
'Chardonnay' white, wine
'Chasselas' ('Royal Muscadine') white, dessert
'Léon Millot' black, wine
'Madeleine Angevine' pale green, dual-purpose
'Madeleine Silvaner' white, wine
'Müller-Thurgau' white, wine
'Noir Hatif de Marseilles' black, wine
'Perlette' black, dual-purpose
'Pirovano 14' red-black, wine
'Précoce de Malingre' white, wine

white grapes

black grapes

'Riesling' white, wine
'Siegerrebe' golden, dual-purpose
'Triomphe d'Alsace' black, wine

Indoor varieties
'Alicante' black, dessert
'Buckland Sweetwater' white, dessert
'Foster's Seedling' white, dessert
'Gros Maroc' black, dessert
'Reine Olga' red-black, dessert
'Schiava Grossa' ('Black Hamburgh') black, dessert
'Seyval Blank' white, wine

life, it is essential to make certain that these supports are solid structures. Posts can be wooden but must be treated against decay. Metal posts are more usual. The wires often have some method of tensioning them so that they can be tightened as they slacken over time. Generally, most systems require one line of posts and wires, but some of the lesser-known methods involve two parallel rows. The various systems train the rods (or fruiting stems) up, along or down the wires.

Pruning and training

There are two basic systems of pruning and training. In one, the fruiting shoots are allowed to develop from scratch each year and are removed after fruiting. This is know as rod renewal. The other is rod-and-spur in which the stems are cut back to one or two buds once the fruit is produced. It is from these spurs that the following year's fruiting growth develops. The method depends on the variety, so it is best to ask your supplier whether the vine is spur-producing or not. The main pruning takes place in the

ABOVE Grapes grown against a wall. Walls provide warmth and help both to protect the blossom and to ripen the fruit.

ABOVE All methods of training involve pruning back the previous year's fruiting growth to one or two buds.

ABOVE Some growers like to leave tying up the vines as late as possible as the fruiting buds develop more easily on arched stems.

middle of winter, but it is also necessary to do a little pruning during the growing season, mainly pinching out growth and unwanted flower bunches.

Pruning cuts

As with most pruning, angle the cuts so that water runs off. On vertical shoots, make the cuts at 30 degrees to the horizontal. On horizontal shoots, cut straight across the stem. The cut should be above a bud, but not so close that you damage the swollen node on which the bud rests. Summer pruning is normally a simple matter of pinching out the soft growth with finger and thumb.

Thinning fruit and leaves

For dessert grapes, it is necessary to thin out the number of grapes in a bunch to produce larger fruit. With a pair of fine-pointed scissors, remove about a quarter to one-third of the fruit from the bunch, leaving the remainder room to develop fully. In autumn, once the fruit begins to ripen, remove any leaves covering the bunches so that sun and light can reach the grapes.

BASIC TECHNIQUES FOR GROWING GRAPES

There are some basic techniques which apply to all methods of growing grapes. Some may not apply to large-scale grape production in commercial vineyards, but the home-grown crops will benefit if you use them.

FOLIAGE THINNNG Once bunches of grapes begin to ripen, it is a good idea to remove some of the leaves that are covering the bunches, to let in sun and light.

SUMMER PRUNING Some vines will grow too vigorously. Any shoots that are not required should be pinched out as soon as they appear.

THINNING THE FRUIT If you want to use the grapes for dessert purposes, it may be necessary to thin them out so that they fill out well.

ROD RENEWAL METHOD The basic pruning cut is to remove the old fruited stem back to one or two buds, from which springs the new fruiting growth.

ROD-AND-SPUR METHOD There comes a point in the life of the vine when the stubs become overcrowded and it is necessary to remove some of them.

The Guyot system

There are in fact two Guyot systems, the single and the double. The double is the most commonly used. The single is very similar but uses only one rod (or fruiting stem) on one side instead of two rods, one on either side. Both methods are widely used for wine grapes grown outside.

Supports

Set well-anchored posts in the ground about 4–5m (13–16ft) apart, with four or five horizontal wires at 30cm (12in) intervals. The bottom wire should be about 45cm (18in) above the soil. The main stem of each individual vine is supported by a wooden stake.

Initial training

Plant a one-year-old vine next to the post in autumn or early winter.

ABOVE The Guyot system is particularly well suited to wine-grape production, which usually gives larger bunches of small grapes, as here.

Around mid-winter, cut it right back to about 15cm (6in) above the ground, retaining two buds. During the summer, allow the main stem to grow and pinch out any side shoots. The following mid-winter, cut back this stem to about 40cm (16in) from the ground, leaving three good strong buds just below the bottom wire. During the following summer, tie in vertically the three shoots that develop from these buds. In mid-winter, gently pull down the two outer shoots to the horizontal and tie them in to the bottom wire on either side of the main stem. Take out the tips of each of these shoots to a bud about 60cm–1m (2–3ft) from the main stem. Cut back the central shoot, leaving three strong buds to develop for the next year.

ABOVE Although vines are normally grown against wires, if only one or two are involved a more permanent support can be used.

ABOVE The Guyot system can be modified for growing dessert grapes under glass in a cool greenhouse or conservatory.

Established pruning

During the following summer, a series of vertical shoots will form on the horizontal arms. Tie these in as they develop and pinch out any side shoots that develop on them. Allow the three buds on the central stem to develop and tie them in, again removing any side shoots that are produced on them.

Fruit is produced on the vertical shoots. Cut out these shoots during the following winter, except for the three central shoots. These are treated the same way as the previous winter, the two lower ones being tied down to the horizontal wires and the central one shortened to three buds. This procedure is repeated every year.

GROWING GRAPES USING THE GUYOT SYSTEM

The Guyot system is very popular among those who grow large quantities of vines for wine-making. It is a relatively simple system and produces good crops, which is the whole purpose of growing grapes in the first place.

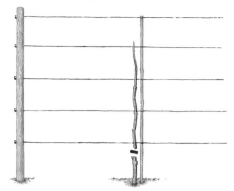

YEAR ONE, WINTER Plant a one-year-old vine and about mid-winter cut back to two buds about 15cm (6in) above the ground.

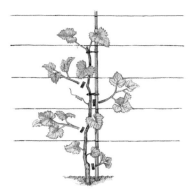

YEAR ONE, SUMMER During the following summer allow the leader to grow. Tie it in and pinch out the side shoots.

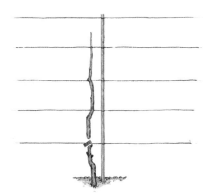

YEAR TWO, WINTER In the following winter cut back the leader to three strong buds just below the bottom wire.

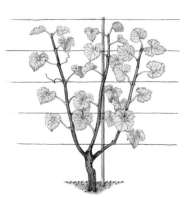

YEAR TWO, SUMMER As the three shoots grow from these buds, tie them in vertically to the stake.

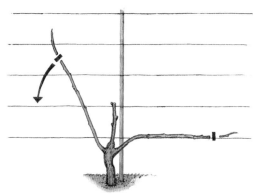

YEAR THREE, WINTER Gently pull down the two outer shoots and tie them horizontally. Cut the central one back to three buds.

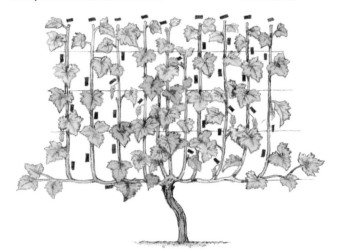

ESTABLISHED PRUNING, SUMMER During the summer tie in the vertical shoots, including the three from the centre, as they develop, pinching out any side shoots. Fruit is produced on the vertical shoots.

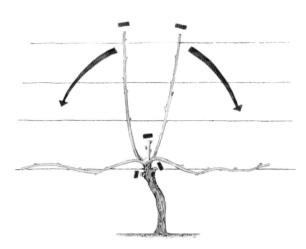

ESTABLISHED PRUNING, WINTER In winter, cut out all the fruited shoots apart from the three central ones. Again, pull down the lower shoots and cut back the central one to three buds. Repeat the last two operations every year.

Grape cordons

Some grape types, especially the dessert varieties, are better pruned using the rod-and-spur system. This method allows rods to grow each year from the same spur as the previous year, rather than being renewed as in the Guyot system. Check when you are buying your grape-vines as to which system is required for growing them. This system is useful for vines grown under glass.

Supports

Using strong supporting posts, run six or more parallel wires between them about 25 cm (10 in) apart, with the bottom one about the same distance above the ground. Place a post or cane into the ground where each vine is to be planted. Some growers like to put tension screws at the end of the wires so that they can be tightened if the wires begin to go slack. Alternatively, the wires can be tightened manually.

GROWING GRAPES AS CORDONS

Growing grapes using the cordon method is popular among home growers. It is relatively labour-intensive, but, on the other hand, not a particularly difficult process. Grape cordons have the advantage of not taking up too much space in the garden – no more than, say, blackberries or loganberries.

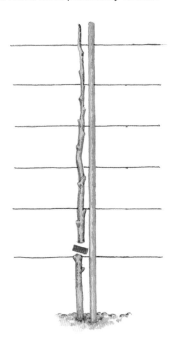

YEAR ONE, WINTER Plant a one-year-old vine in early to mid-winter and cut it back just below the bottom wire to two strong buds.

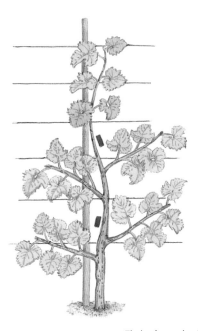

YEAR ONE, SUMMER Tie in the main shoot and tie in any laterals level with the wires. Pinch out any side shoots that form on these stems and any side shoots not level with the wires.

ABOVE Dessert grapes are best pruned using a rod-and-spur system, which is suitable for greenhouses as well as growing in the open.

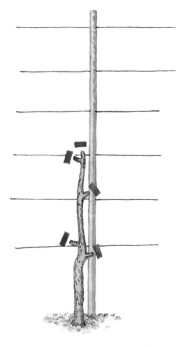

YEAR TWO, WINTER The next winter, prune back all the laterals to just one bud. Cut back the new growth of the main shoot to half.

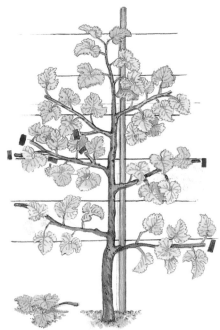

YEAR TWO, SUMMER Continue the previous summer's treatment, except now prune back any sub-laterals to one leaf and take out the tips of the laterals themselves.

Initial pruning

Plant a one-year-old vine in early to mid-winter, and cut it back to two strong buds roughly at the level of the bottom wire. During the following summer, allow the main shoot to develop and tie it in. Allow any side shoots to develop that are level with the wires, so that one can be trained on either side. Pinch out any others. Also pinch out any side shoots that form on the stems that are retained. The following winter, prune back the laterals heavily to just one or two buds on each. Cut back the main shoot to about half its length, choosing a bud on the other side of the stem to the previous year's cut. Continue this cycle until the vine has rods trained on to all the wires.

Established pruning

The bottom arms will be established before the top ones have been produced. The procedure is basically the same as the initial training. Pinch out all side shoots on the lateral arms in summer. If the grapes are for dessert use, reduce the number of bunches of flowers to one on each so that only one bunch of grapes develops on each arm. More can be allowed on wine grapes, as the berries do not need to grow so large. Pinch back the tips of the laterals to about 60cm (2ft) or longer if they are wine grapes, in which case tip them just beyond the last bunch of flowers. The following winter, cut back all rods to just one or two buds. Gently bend the top of the main stem to the horizontal and tie it down. This will encourage the buds on the lower rods to produce shoots. Once the buds start to burst, release the top of the main stem and tie it in vertically again. Repeat this procedure every year.

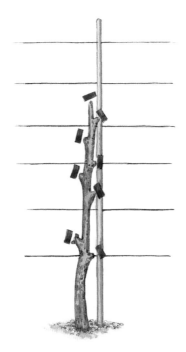

YEAR THREE, WINTER Continue to cut back each winter all laterals to one or two buds and the new growth of the leader by about half.

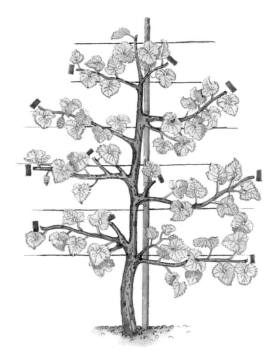

SUBSEQUENT YEARS Repeat both previous summer and winter pruning until the leader consists of mature wood right up to the top wire. From now on, cut the leader back to about six leaves each summer.

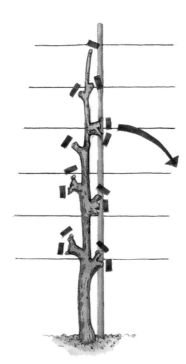

ESTABLISHED PRUNING, WINTER Each winter after becoming established, cut back all main laterals and the leader to one or two buds. Gently pull the top half of the leader down to the horizontal and tie it in.

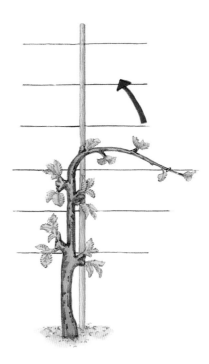

ESTABLISHED PRUNING, SPRING In spring, once the bottom buds start to break, take the leader up to the vertical. In summer cut back the laterals and leader to about 60cm (2ft) and all side shoots to one leaf.

Single curtain system

This is a system widely used in commerce for spur-pruned vines. It is less labour-intensive than other methods as there is no tying-in.

Supports

Insert sturdy posts into the ground at 4–5m (13–16ft) intervals. Stretch five wires tightly between them, spaced 45cm (18in) apart. Insert a post or cane in the ground where the vine is to be planted.

Initial training

Plant one-year-old vines against each of the canes and tie them in. In the first winter, cut the stems hard back to about 15cm (6in), leaving at least one strong bud. In summer, tie in the new leader as it develops. Next winter, cut back the leader again, removing about half of the previous year's growth. Tie in the new leader as it develops. During the third winter, remove all laterals on the main stem except for two just below the top wire (or one lateral and the leader if there are not two well-placed laterals). Bend these outwards and tie them down to the top wire. Next summer shoots will appear along these laterals that will initially be upright, then hang down. Allow them to develop at about 30cm (12in) intervals along the laterals, removing any in between. Also pinch out any side shoots that appear on them, as well as any shoots that appear on the underside of the main laterals.

Established pruning

From now on the main pruning should be carried out around mid-winter, before the sap rises. Cut back all the hanging shoots to one or two upward-facing buds. Remove completely any downward-pointing ones. Next, allow one shoot to develop on the previous year's spurs and remove any others.

GROWING GRAPES USING THE SINGLE CURTAIN SYSTEM

This is a system that, like that of using cordons, produces a rod-and-spur system, but there is not as much labour required.

This means that it is easier for large numbers of vines. The basic principles are the same as for other methods.

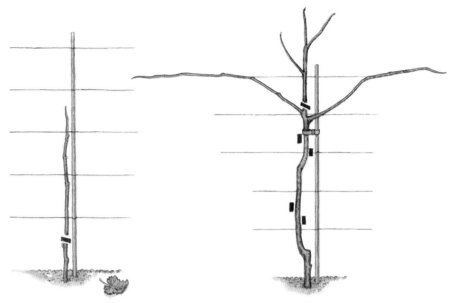

YEARS ONE AND TWO, WINTER AND SUMMER Start with a one-year-old vine planted in winter and cut through the leader about 15cm (6in) above ground-level. In summer, tie in the new leader as it develops. The following winter, cut back the leader again, this time removing about half of the previous year's growth. Again, tie in the leader as it develops. Continue this process until the top wires are reached.

YEAR THREE, WINTER In winter remove all the laterals on the main stem except for two just below the top wire. Bend these out and tie to the top wire.

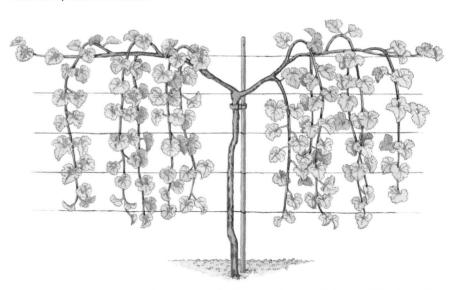

YEAR THREE, SUMMER In the summer, side shoots on these two laterals will develop and hang down. Allow them to develop at 30cm (12in) intervals. Pinch out any side shoots that appear on them, as well as any that appear on the underside of the main laterals. Once established, prune in the winter, cutting back all the hanging shoots to one or two upward-facing buds and allowing one shoot to develop on the previous year's spurs.

Double curtain system

Also known as the Geneva Double Curtain, this was the original curtain system from which the single system and other minor variations were developed. The advantage for the home grower is that it saves space. Although each row is slightly wider, the method allows more vines to be grown in the same length of row.

Supports

There are two possible methods of wirework. One involves two parallel rows of wire stretched taut between sturdy posts. The rows are about 60cm (2ft) apart and the wires are held 1.5m (5ft) from the ground. The alternative is to use one row of posts, each with a crossbar at the top from which the two rows of wires are suspended. Posts to support the vines are placed down the middle of the two rows (or at either side/to one side of the single row) at each planting position, roughly 1.2m (4ft) apart.

ABOVE In cooler countries dessert grapes are best grown under glass, where a good crop can be expected.

Initial training

This is exactly the same as for the single system, except that the top laterals are first tied across the rows and then turned in opposite directions along the wires. You will first need to plant one-year-old vines against each of the planting posts. The first winter, cut the stem hard back to about 15cm (6in) above ground-level, leaving at least one strong bud. In the summer, tie in the new leader as it develops. In the second winter, cut back the leader again to remove about half of the previous year's growth. Again tie in the new leader as it develops. During the third winter, remove all laterals that have developed on the main stem except for two just below the wire (or one lateral and the leader if there are not two conveniently placed laterals). Bend these outwards until they meet the wires and then turn them along the wires, one in each direction, tying them down to the wires. The next summer, shoots will appear along these laterals that will initially be upright, then hang down. Allow them to develop at about 30cm (12in) intervals along the laterals, removing any in between. Also pinch out any side shoots that appear on them, as well as any shoots that appear on the underside of the main laterals.

Established pruning

The main pruning should be carried out around mid-winter, before the sap rises. Cut back all the hanging shoots to one or two upward-facing buds. Remove completely any downward-pointing ones. The next summer, allow one shoot to develop on the previous year's spurs and remove any others. Repeat these procedures every winter and summer.

GROWING GRAPES USING THE DOUBLE CURTAIN SYSTEM

This system is very similar to the previous method, the single curtain system, except that it is spread over two rows about 60cm (2ft) apart. This allows more vines to be grown in a small space than with the single method.

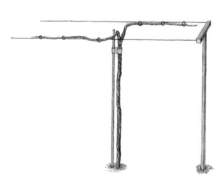

YEAR THREE, WINTER The vine is grown in the same way as for the single curtain system except that each lateral is bent in an L-shape and spread along alternate wires.

ESTABLISHED PRUNING Again the system is the same as for the single curtain sytem, with the side shoots now hanging from the laterals in two rows instead of one.

Glossary

Acclimatization The need to allow new trees and bushes to get used to cooler or moister conditions if they have been grown under cover.

Adventitious buds Dormant buds waiting to be stimulated into growth.

Aerial roots Roots that emerge from trunks or other stems above ground.

Apex The tip of a stem or shoot.

Axil The upper angle that a leaf stalk makes with the stem.

Axillary buds Buds that are formed in the axils, i.e. between the leaf stalk and the stem.

Bare-rooted Plants that are bought or otherwise acquired that are not in a container, and have had the soil removed from their roots.

Basal Leaves or shoots growing at the base of a plant.

Blind shoots Shoots that have failed to produce a flower.

Branch leader The main shoot of a branch that is increasing its length.

Break Shoots, leaves or blossom starting to grow from their buds.

Brutting The partial breaking of shoots on a cobnut tree.

Bush tree A compact tree on a short trunk.

Central leader The main, central shoot of a tree or shrub.

Cordon A single-stem method of growing fruit trees and bushes in a confined area.

Crown The main part of the tree above the trunk.

Defoliation Loss or removal of leaves.

Die-back The dying of shoots or other wood from either the tip or point of cutting.

Double cordon A two-stemmed cordon forming a "U"-shape.

Dwarfing rootstock Rootstock that produces small trees.

Espalier A decorative form of training with tiered layers of side branches either side of a central trunk.

Fan A decorative training method where branches radiate out from a short trunk.

Framework The permanent structure of branches.

Graft Joining one type of plant on to another plant's rootstock.

Graft union The junction between the top (scion) and the bottom (rootstock) of a grafted plant.

Internode The piece of shoot between two nodes, i.e. between two side shoots, leaves or buds.

Lateral Side shoot.

Leader A main stem.

Long-arm pruners Secateurs (pruners) on a long pole that can be operated from the lower end while reaching up into trees or shrubs.

Long-handled pruners Secateurs (pruners) with long handles for cutting thicker stems.

Maiden A tree in its first year.

Maiden whip A tree in its first year without as yet any side shoots.

Mulch A ground-covering material to conserve moisture and prevent weed growth.

Multiple cordon A cordon that has three or more vertical stems.

Petiole A leaf stalk.

Pinching out To prune by pinching out a soft shoot between finger and thumb.

Pleaching Training adjacent trees so that their branches are interwoven to form a screen.

Pruning saw A small, sharp saw designed for pruning.

Replacement shoot A strong shoot that is used to replace the one being removed.

Rootball The collection of roots, still with their soil, as found in a container or when a plant is dug up.

Rootstock The rooted section of a grafted plant.

Rubbing out Removal of soft shoots by rubbing with the hand.

Scion The upper part of a grafted plant, from which the plant takes most of its character.

Secateurs (pruners) Hand tools that are somewhat like strong scissors for pruning thin stems.

Semi-standard A tree that is halfway between a bush tree and a full standard. The clear trunk is usually about 1.2m (4ft).

Shears A cutting tool rather like large scissors for trimming hedges.

Side shoot A shoot that appears on the side of a more major stem.

Snag A short length of stem between a bud and a pruning cut.

Spindle bush A small fruit tree in which the branches are artificially lowered to the horizontal.

Spur A short shoot that bears the fruit buds.

Spur-pruning Pruning to encourage the development of spurs.

Spur-thinning Reducing the number of spurs in one place when they become overcrowded.

Standard A full-size tree usually with a clear trunk.

Stopping Pinching out a shoot to make it branch out.

Stub The remaining portion of a shoot when the rest has been cut off.

Sub-lateral A side shoot on a shoot that is already a side shoot itself.

Sucker (1) Shoots that arise from around the base of a plant or from its roots (often from the rootstock of a grafted plant). (2) Vigorous vertical growth from the branches of a fruit tree.

Terminal The tip of a shoot.

Thinning Reducing the number of shoots, spurs or fruits.

Tip-bearing Fruit trees that bear mainly at the ends of their shoots.

Tip-pruning Removing the tip of a shoot to make it branch out.

Trunk The main stem of a tree.

Wirework Wires that are attached on posts used to support plants.

Index

Acknowledgements

The Publisher would like to thank the following gardens and garden owners for kindly allowing photography to take place on their premises:

Andrew Mikolajski, Northamptonshire; Bedgebury Pinetum, Kent; Batsford Arboretum, Gloucestershire; Brogdale Horticultural Trust, Faversham, Kent; Chenies Manor, Buckinghamshire; Chiffchaffs, Dorset; East Lambrook Manor, Somerset; Elsing Hall, Norfolk; Headland Garden, Cornwall; Fiona Henley Design; Lamport Hall,

Northamptonshire; Merrist Wood, Surrey; Pine Lodge Gardens, Cornwall; Renishaw Hall, Sheffield; RHS Chelsea Flower Show 2004; RHS Hyde Hall, Essex; RHS Gardens Rosemoor, Devon; RHS Gardens Wisley, Surrey; Rodmarton Manor, Cirencester; Spinners, Devon; Westonbirt Arboretum, Gloucestershire; Wollerton Old Hall, Shropshire; Writtle College, Essex; Wyken Hall, Suffolk; Yalding Organic Gardens, Kent

A special thank you goes to STIHL Ltd. who kindly lent some of the tools and equipment used in the

book. A list of worldwide suppliers that stock Stihl products can be found on their website:
www.stihl.com

The Publisher would like to thank the following people for acting as models in photography sessions:

Jeff Clayton; Nick Robinson; Peter Sedgewick; Robin Whitehead; Stephen Coling

The Publisher would also like to thank the following picture libraries for kindly allowing their images to be reproduced in this book:

t = top b = bottom c = centre
l = left r = right

Science Photo Library:
43tl (Dan Sams); 43tr (Keith Seaman); 43bl (M F Merlet); 44b (Ed Young); 46bl (Roger Standen); 46br (K Wise); 50bl (John Marshall); 85bl (Helmut Partsch)

The Garden Picture Library:
22bl (Ellen Rooney); 52b (John Glover); 53tl (John Glover)

Garden World Images: 25tr; 44t; 84tr

Holt Images: 24t; 54t; 58c; 85br